WISH YOU WERE HERE

*Cover Pictures: 1. The Milton "Localized" Series No. 413 (above)
and 2. No. 414 (below)*

3. Jersey Fisherman Making Crab Pots
(Photo G. Bridle, Jersey
Printed in Germany)

Wish you were here ...

A Holiday History of Jersey seen through picture postcards

John Le Dain

SEAFLOWER BOOKS

Published in 2002 by
SEAFLOWER BOOKS
1 The Shambles
Bradford on Avon
Wiltshire   BA15 1JS

www.ex-librisbooks.co.uk

Designed by Seaflower Books

Printed by Cromwell Press
Trowbridge, Wiltshire

ISBN 1 903341 12 4

Acknowledgements
I am indebted to members of the Postcard Study Group
of the Bibliography Section of the Société Jersiaise, and
particulary to David Le Maistre, who gave of his time and
most generously allowed my to plug a few gaps in this
book by letting me take copies of five postcards from his
extensive collection and allowing me to reproduction
here. They are Nos. 46, 84, 192, 243 and the picture of
Harry on page 46. David also permitted me to reproduce
some of the messages written on postcards in his
collection.
Thanks also to Brian Ahier Read for proof-reading and
offering useful comments. And, finally, thanks to all those
correspondents whose holiday jottings are quoted in these
pages.

Contents...

Grève-de-Lecq Bay, Jersey.

4.Sent to E.H. Pope Esq, Bromley, Kent and postmarked June 25/13 [June 25th, 1913]

Have had another topping day. We walked over to Plémont this morning and then on to Grève de Lecq whence we turned our steps homeward. Reckon we must have covered something like 20 miles & as there is a whist drive and dance on tonight expect to feel tired. We wandered into town last night and purchased a small bottle of D.O.M. so indulge in a nightcap when we get upstairs. I find it helps H.S. from snoring.'

L.C.

Introduction

This book began life some years ago when I wandered into an Antiques Fair in Cirencester. One of the stall-holders was a picture postcard dealer who stood over trays upon trays full of old postcards, including a large section devoted to places, especially the British Isles, organised under county headings. At the end of the A-Z sequence was Yorkshire, followed by the Channel Islands, detached here as they are on the map. I'd never purchased old postcards before and was only vaguely aware that there was such a pursuit as postcard collecting. I found a couple of interesting Jersey items – one an early view of Grève de Lecq (see opposite), the other a composite view (see overleaf). When I turned them over I found myself riveted by the messages. Each postcard offers a double-faceted glimpse of Jersey at the time of its sending – a view of the island and a glimpse of the sender's holiday experience.

✳

The first British postcards were placed on sale in October 1870, a year after their inauguration in the Austro-Hungarian empire. At first they were entirely plain, with the address to be written on one side, together with a halfpenny stamp for posting (rather than 1d for a letter) and the message on the reverse. These were officially produced and the Post Office insisted that only these could be posted at the halfpenny rate, whilst privately printed cards were liable to the full penny rate. Meanwhile, on the Continent, post-cards soon began bearing illustrations; the advent of the holiday postcard had begun.

In Britain, the postage penalty continued until 1894 and in 1902 the address and message were permitted to be written on the same side as the stamp, freeing the reverse for the picture illustration. By this time German printers were well ahead of the game and cornered much of the production of British published postcards – the reason so many early British cards were printed in Saxony and Bavaria. Thus the postcard era in Britain properly began in 1902, a fact which is neatly and superbly illustrated in a recent book, *Postcard Century* (Thames and Hudson: 2000), by artist

5.

'Willrose
43, Kensington Place

A greeting from an old pal to remind you of the good old days!!! Have been attempting to visit you since Xmas to thank you for flowers. Shall manage it one day. It is glorious here (once you arrive). Plenty of sunshine & shops full of food. Can recommend this place if you want a carefree holiday.
Love to George, the Capt. & Self.

Grace'

This composite card, made up of views of St. Aubin, the Harbour, Vinchelez Lane, St. Brelade's Church and Fisherman's Chapel and Corbière Rocks and Lighthouse, was sent to Mrs Davies of Bournemouth. Grace's card is postmarked 2nd July 1946, the first holiday season after Liberation. She had apparently visited Jersey before the war, in 'the good old days', and seems extremely happy to be back. The comment that 'shops full of food' is made against the experience of strict rationing in mainland Britain at this time.

and postcard collector Tom Phillips, in which he depicts each year of the century with a selection of picture postcards and their messages. This beautifully produced book has raised the homely pastime of postcard collecting to new heights – is it art, social history, biography? Surely, a bit of all these.

There are many books which are collections of postcards focusing on particular places – Stenlake Publications of Ayrshire, for example, currently has a list of several hundred titles. But *Postcard Century* was the first book, to my knowledge, which gave equal attention to the postcard messages as well as the illustrations.

⁂

Postcard collecting as a hobby rapidly grew in popularity. People sent postcards to their friends not simply to convey a message but in order to boost that friend's postcard collection; (see example overleaf) and they would often expect a postcard in return. People accumulated postcard albums and swapped duplicates with their friends. Even today, postcards of the Edwardian era are more commonplace than those of the interwar period – not necessarily because more were sent, which is unlikely, but because more were collected and saved for posterity. More people on holiday had cameras after the First World War so they accumulated photograph albums as holiday

souvenirs rather than the more impersonal postcard collections.

Probably the majority of old Jersey postcards in circulation today were sent by holidaymakers to family and friends at home, or, more often, simply purchased as holiday souvenirs. In the latter case the cards will be without a written message, which I always find a disappointment. But a significant minority of Jersey postcards were sent and received locally, within the island. Postcards became a means of communication for locals – some of the messages in this case are wonderfully intriguing, though you begin to feel slightly uncomfortable on reading them, as though you were snooping into the domestic details of the lives of strangers. But they are irresistible all the same.

⁂

In the days of a super-efficient postal service, with several collections and deliveries daily, people used postcards to transmit brief written messages, just as we use the telephone today. Or perhaps I should say text messaging by mobile phone which, since its inception in 1999, has increased in popularity at a phenomenal rate. There are interesting parallels between communication by postcard and text messaging. The latter medium tends to favour a kind of shorthand, exemplified by one of the many little books offering instruction, entitled

1891. Environs of Jersey
The natural bridge of the Petit Becquet   G. F.

One more for your collection.
With love from
FG
May 1903

6. Environs of Jersey:
The natural bridge of the Petit Becquet, between Grève de Lecq and Plémont, but not easy to find.

'One more for your collection. With love from FG May 1903' and sent to Master Eady – see address side reproduced below.

This card is attributed to 'Collection Germain fils aîné, Saint-Malo.'

CARTE POSTALE

Ce côté est exclusivement réservé à l'adresse

Master Roland H. Eady
4 Windsor Villas
Val Pleasant

Local

'RUUP4IT?', which translates as 'Are You Up For It?' which, for most of us, probably needs further translation.

Postcard writing is, perhaps, not quite as radical a literary form as text messaging, but normal rules of grammar, and certainly of punctuation, usually do not apply. In the absence of commas and full stops sentences tend to run together so that postcard correspondents often seem to have been in a hurry. Which of course they were, dutifully writing to all and sundry at home when what they would perhaps rather have been doing was enjoying their holiday.

✳

However, the focus of this book is the postcards which tourists sent home, and what the views and the messages reveal about the story of Jersey as a holiday destination. The development of tourism is as much an aspect of our social history as education or women's rights or anything else. But tourism is predominantly a happy subject, a point that is repeatedly emphasised in the messages people write on postcards.

✳

Tourism in Jersey first developed during the Napoleonic Wars, at the beginning of the nineteenth century, when continental travel became difficult for the British. The first guide book for tourists – Stead's *A Picture of Jersey, or Stranger's Companion through that Island*, was published in 1809, and this was followed by many more. Such guide books sought to direct the visitor around the island, and provide a commentary on places seen and on history and culture. Such books began appearing before the age of photography and were illustrated, if at all, with engravings – often rather inaccurate representations of local scenes. The first Jersey postcards appeared in 1897 and the number of cards and range of subjects available grew rapidly thereafter.

As their target audience, the postcard manfacturers probably had in mind the holidaymakers whose numbers increased steadily towards the end of the nineteenth century and the early years the twentieth. But one wonders how many tourists would choose a postcard of the Female Orphans' Home, or Dr Barnardo's Home for Little Boys at Gorey, such institutions not constituting priority holiday destinations. Others were produced to promote individual businesses: hotels, cafés, shops. And yet others were made from pictures taken by itinerant photographers who often specialised in snapping groups – most often at the outset of a charabanc outing, or in front of a hotel. Copies of these pictures would then be available next day for persons in the group to purchase.

The advent of the postcard coincided with the growing popularity of tourism in Jersey. Indeed, tourism rivalled agriculture as the island's biggest employer and revenue earner until the rise of the finance industry in the 1970s which, by the close of the twentieth century, appeared to dominate Jersey's economic life. The inexorable increase in population, the inflated price of houses and rental accommodation, the demise of agriculture and the ransacking of St Helier to erect yet more offices for banks, as well as the rapidly diminishing tourism industry, may all in large part be blamed on the mushrooming finance industry.

Offshore finance is where the big money is, so all else suffers as a result. One day the bubble will burst, as bubbles always do; perhaps then Jersey will see a revival of tourism. But at the beginning of the twenty-first century the outlook appears bleak – hotels and guest houses are going down like ninepins, beach cafés and tourist attractions are closing, even car hire firms are disappearing.

It seems a shame... or am I just being nostalgic, having personally enjoyed holidays in Jersey every year since I can remember – since 1945, in fact. A place which has given so much pleasure to so many people for so many years must be special. Well, of course, Jersey is special, with its golden beaches, rocky headlands, wooded valleys, delicious countryside. And all those thousands of holidays and the

generations of visitors who have enjoyed them have surely lent Jersey a kind of aura, or is it simply that it's such a beautiful island?

There is no reference guide to the wealth of Jersey postcards, an untold number, which has been produced over the past century or so. Perhaps, by now, some have disappeared without trace. However, there are many avid collectors of Jersey postcards, perhaps none more so than members of the Postcard Study Group of the Bibliography Section of the Société Jersiaise, the local antiquarian society, who are engaged in the monumental task of cataloguing Jersey postcards. Data derived from each member's collection is pooled for the purpose of establishing a definitive listing. Such a catalogue will be a considerable contribution to the historical record, a record of a subject which is by its nature ephemeral and fleeting. Text messaging, perhaps the postcard's contemporary equivalent, will leave no such record, as all the content is lost in the ether, so that a literary form is developing which future historians will be unable to study.

When the idea for this book began to take shape, in early 2000, I started seriously collecting Jersey postcards, In August that year I spent a day at the

Picture Postcard Show held annually at the Royal Agricultural Halls in Westminster. This prestigious and spacious venue plays host to well over a hundred exhibitors, many from overseas but the majority from around Britain. Stallholders often have a speciality but nearly all have a good selection of 'topographicals', or 'topo' cards, as they are known, i.e. views of places. And, within this, there is always a section on the Channel Islands, sometimes split into Jersey, Guernsey and Sark (Alderney rarely turns up) or otherwise lumped together with the Isles of Scilly and even Lundy Island. I spent a lot of dosh that day and began to assemble a respectable collection. Like the Provincial Booksellers Fairs Association, the Postcard Traders Association organises a programme of fairs around the country; I've attended one or two of these locally. Now, with a mere 500 or so Jersey postcards in my possession, I feel I have a representative collection. That is, a collection which relates something of the story of the evolution of the Jersey postcard and, in association, the Jersey holiday.

I visited the 2001 London Show and managed to spend a little less that I had the year before, though I came away with far fewer cards. This was because most of the cards I saw I already had, and most of the more expensive ones I'd resisted buying the year before. Certain cards turn up again and again

– those tend to be cheaper, naturally. But for the purpose of this enquiry, the common cards are not necessarily less interesting. Indeed, being sent more often they could be said to be more typical. The rarer, relatively expensive items are essential to the pure collector and, I have to admit, I have coveted particular cards and ignored my wife's taunts of my becoming a 'postcard anorak'. The most I've ever paid for a card is £35. (I hope my wife doesn't read this). That was at the 2001 London Show. It was for a card I'd seen the year before – perhaps the same copy – but was deterred from purchasing it by its high price. So I bought it, without a discount (I did try) and then, two stalls along and ten minutes later, found the same card priced at £18! I registered my displeasure with the original vendor and wished him a happy retirement (I hope he detected my note of sarcasm). But I remember feeling smug, at the 2000 Show, when I found a card priced at £5 which I'd just bought elsewhere for 50p. Having made these comments about pricing, it comes as a surprise to discover how consistent prices generally are, which points up how knowledgeable many dealers are with a commodity which seems to offer an almost infinite range.

All the images in this book are reproduced in black and white simply because the originals were printed in

black ink, or sepia ink, on white card. If originals were in colour, that is stated. Colour postcards are as old as monochrome but they were not based on colour photographs – the technology for doing so had not been developed, or was too expensive. They were often black and white images which had been tinted and occasionally the odd choice of colour produced bizarre results. Indeed, until the 1930s, black and white postcards were printed by a process known as photogravure; they were not based on photographs screened to produce a pattern of differently sized dots in order to create an illusion of shades of grey. The advent of photographic cards was a matter of pride to the manufacturers and the legend 'This is a Real Photograph' was often proudly proclaimed on the message side. These were indeed real photographs and did not go through the screening process which for many years now has been a preliminary to offset litho printing. So, first it was photogravure, then real photographs, then screened photographs printed by offset litho.

Early postcards vary hugely in quality – some present clear and well lit images whilst others are rather poor – woolly grey images lacking detail other than light and dark areas which represent sky and land respectively. Even with modern computer scanning and image enhance-ment capability it is still difficult to improve much on these inferior images.

Postcards based on black and white photographs were replaced by those based on colour photographs in the late 1960s/early 1970s. The monochrome postcards which generally predate 1970, so are less familiar to us today, perhaps best illustrate the heyday of tourism in the island. Besides, the publisher, who is also the compiler of this book, can't really justify the expense of colour printing.

✳

When I began assembling my growing collection of Jersey postcards I put them into broad chronological categories: pre-First World War, between the Wars and post-Second World War. Then, with this book in mind, a more clearly defined and useful classification seemed appropriate – thematic rather than chronological – the chapter headings on the Contents page speak for themselves.

All the postcard images in this book are from my own collection except where stated. And for the anoraks – sorry, collectors – amongst you, I have given publication details.

John Le Dain
2002

Arrival

Steam ships began replacing sail around the beginning of the nineteeth century. The greater frequency and improved punctuality of sea connections between Jersey and the mainland enabled a steady increase in the number of holiday visitors and to the development of tourism as a local industry.

There were sailings from a variety of ports on England's south coast; there was even a direct sailing from London which took 26 hours. However, the two main routes were the Great Western Railway (GWR) from Weymouth and London and the London and South Western Railway (LSWR) – later the Southern Railway (SR) – from Southampton. However, by the 1920s these two companies ran their services in conjunction and sponsored joint advertising of their 'Daily Service between England & Jersey by Large Twin-Screw and Turbine Steamers'.

A succession of boats served these two companies which, after rail nationalisation in 1948, became British Railways, then Sealink. Whether sailing from Weymouth or Southampton, the journey was a long one. Excitement at the prospect of the voyage was often tempered by anticipation of a rough crossing and seasickness. Many postcards home start with a report on the crossing and correspondents often remark, 'Dreadful crossing, but it was worth it!'

Air services began in 1933, when small biplanes from England landed on the beach at West Park prior to the opening Jersey Airport in 1937. The Occupation stopped tourism in its tracks but the German occupiers at least improved the airport by lengthening its runways whilst they were in residence.

After 1945 air services grew steadily but the cheaper boat services held their own and began to fight back with the introduction of high-speed hydrofolis in the 1970s and, subsequently, of spacious, car-carrying catamarans.

To Leslie Cole in Southampton, post-marked 194?:

'Had a rough crossing but managed to sleep and keep fit until after Guernsey – then, oh dear, I <u>had</u> it! Shall return by air on Tuesday.'

(F.F. Phototone Series)

☀

Message on card sent to Mrs V Isaacson, 1956:

'Dear Nan,
Just to let you know we have recovered from a very rough crossing here, it was terrible. The sun is shining today and we hope to bathe later.'

☀

9. The SS *Roebuck*, launched in 1897, struck a rock off Jersey on July 19th, 1911. The ship ran aground on Les Caines reef just to the south-west of Beauport. Interestingly, this postcard is postmarked August 11th, 1911, barely three weeks after the event, which means that some enterprising postcard manufacturer must have processed this card very quickly. It was sent to a Mr Harrison in Exmouth and the message reads:

'We arrived at Jersey safely last night at 9.30, there was no morning boat. We were caught in a fearful thunderstorm last Saturday and this morning it is very showery but fearfully hot.
                    Love from Daisy.'

(J.W. & S.)

☀

7. The London & South West Railway Company's SS *Alberta* passing Elizabeth Castle. (Pitt Series No.64)

8. The arrival of Great Western Railway Company's SS *Roebuck* reversing into St. Helier Harbour. (F.F. Photogravure Series)

9.

10. View of St Helier Harbour taken from Pier Road. The person who collected this postcard noted the date 16th/17th September, 1903, and we can see that we are very much still in the age of sail. La Folie Inn can be seen middle left.
(JW & C 401)

⁂

11. Queen Victoria Statue, St Helier Harbour. This monument to Queen Victoria was unveiled in 1890 but was later moved to what became known as Victoria Park (Pierson Road, formerly Triangle Park) to make way for the bus station.
In evidence here are plenty of sailing ships as well as the sheds which currently house the Maritime Museum and the Occupation Tapestry.
(Photostyle Series No. 24)

12. Embarking at Jersey.
Unidentified ship, possibly the SS *Lydia*, unloading passengers at the Albert Pier. Hotels often provided their own coaches to collect guests arriving at the harbour. The coach being pulled by the two white horses, middle foreground, is from the Pomme D'Or.
(F.F. Jersey)

⁂

A message well to the point:

'Arrived well
Safe trip
Not sick
Weather grand'

St-Hellier Harbour Jersey.

JW&C 401

10.

11.

12.

13. View of the Harbour and Elizabeth Castle from Pier Road. This card is postmarked 1st August 1952 so is dated some 50 years after no. 10. Visitors now arrived in a new generation of ferries like those opposite, though the vessel with the single funnel moored at Albert Quay cannot be one of these. This card was sent to Mr & Mrs Adams of Orpington, Kent:

'Having a very good holiday here. Saw the Battle of Flowers yesterday and it was marvellous. Everything parched as they have had very little rain since April.'

(Photo Precision Ltd., St Albans)

Message from a card sent in 1951 to Miss Ross of Grimsby:

'Well we have arrived safely after a very good crossing. There are quite a few young people staying but some are most peculiar!! Yesterday was heavenly, we spent the afternoon in & out of the sea listening to the cricket.

Cheerio, Alice Walker'

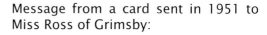

Message on card sent to Mrs Morish of Newport, Monmouthshire (undated):

'Dear Mum & Dad

I was sick as a dog on the way over but it is great here now. There is some fine wine I can bring you back for a present.

From Harry'

The Harbour, & Elizabeth Castle, St Helier, Jersey.

13.

14. S.S. *Isle of Jersey*. This ship worked the Southampton-Channel Islands route for the Southern Railway and entered service in 1930.
(The R.A. [Postcards] Ltd., London, E.C.4)

15. S.S. *Isle of Guernsey*. Sister ship to the Isle of Jersey, also entered service in 1930. The *Isle of Sark* (not pictured) joined them in 1932.
(A.G. Le Moer, Montrose, St. Martins, Jersey)

16. Jersey Airport was opened in 1937 but, from 1933, passenger aircraft flying from England landed and took off from the beach at West Park which, of course, depended upon the state of the tide. This view shows a number of Dragon Rapides, a twin-propellor biplane.

✳

17. Dragon Rapide at Jersey Airport. This view, and no. 18, gives a good impression of the original airport building, with its attractive wedding cake structure supporting the control tower at its summit. This card is post-marked 14th August, 1939, and is addressed to Mrs Keech of Battersea, London:

'Dear Mum,
Arrived here 10.30am having caught 9 o'clock 'plane from Southampton. Flew in beautiful weather – quite an experience. Hope everything is well.
Love, Charles'

(Valentine's)

18. Like the message written on no.17, the message here reflects something of the novelty of flying:
To Mrs Page of Leeds, Yorkshire:

'This is the type of plane we came here in [Dakota DC3]. Good job it wasn't yesterday, the weather grounded them for most of the day. Apparently it has been a bad season altogether, and the locals don't promise anything better. Today the sky is overcast, and there is a rougher sea running, quite a picture really. The hotel is quite good, clean, and the food well cooked.
Love, Vera'

(B.B. London)

✳

Message on card sent in 1934 to Mrs A Peck of Hackney, London:

'Dear Mother,
Arrived OK. If you ever think of coming take my tip come by air.
Yours Bill'

16.

JERSEY AIRPORT.

G.6103.

"PHOTO BY JERSEY EVENING POST"

17.

JERSEY AIRPORT.

18.

19. Wings over Mont Orgueil
This is a Heron aircraft belonging to Jersey Airlines. The photograph is most likely faked, the image of the aircraft being superimposed on the aerial view of Gorey, but done quite convincingly.
(No attribution but the message 'This is a real Photograph', which probably does not tell the whole truth)

Message from a postcard sent in 1952, from Roger Thrabel to Miss Jahn of Lincoln:

'Dear Elfrida,
We enjoyed our first flight and found it a most comfortable journey only $1\frac{1}{2}$ hours from Northolt... The weather is very good and we are enjoying our holiday here very much.'

Message to Mr & Mrs Goodfellow of Wembley Park, Middlesex in 1937:

'Having a lovely time. Flying is great. Only 3 hours from door to door.'

Where to Stay

An advertisement for the Royal Yacht Hotel in the 1920s claimed it to be 'The Oldest Established Hotel in the Island … Facing Sea and Harbour, and Most Centrally Situated for Railway Stations,' and that 'Excursion Cars start from Hotel Twice Daily during the Season; Hotel Omnibus Meets Mail Boats.'

Many of the earliest hotels were, unsurprisingly, situated close to the harbour. All the larger establishments provided excursion cars and met new arrivals at the quay.

The opening of hotels and boarding houses, some purpose-built but others converted from older buildings, facilitated the development of tourism from the early nineteenth century onwards.

Every establishment sought to advertise its own unique features, sometimes with a little exaggeration. St. Brelade's Bay Hotel claims that: 'This is the only Hotel in the Channel Islands affording facilities for Sea Bathing, which may be enjoyed at any state of the tide from Sands in front of the house.' The Stag's Head Hotel, at Snow Hill, a busy intersection, was 'Centrally Situated. Every Room in Front of House with outlook down Main Street of Town.' And the Halkett Hotel: 'Visitors arriving at the Height of the Season and desiring a degree of quietude (more or less unobtainable in some parts of the Town just then) can be assured of finding it at this Establishment.'

There have long been as many hotels outside St. Helier as within the town, though many of the largest have been in town. Between the wars hotels began to offer the attractions of a swimming pool, a billiards room, a ping pong room, a London Dance Band and Cabaret, 'Young Company' and 'Small Tables' (as opposed to tables shared with other guests).

Holiday Camps first appeared in the 1920s but now both Portelet and Plémont are history.

20. Grand Hotel and West End Promenade: This Edwardian view from the top of the slipway opposite the Grand shows its windows well protected with stripy blinds against the sun. The railings behind the seated holiday-makers enclose the railway track which ran to St. Aubin and beyond. The up-market Grand, with its advantageous position and views across St. Aubin's Bay, was commandeered by the Germans during the Occupation. (Pitt Series No. 19)

The Somerville Hotel, St Aubin's, Jersey.

21. The Somerville Hotel at St. Aubin's, another of Jersey more prestigious establishments.

**THE ROYAL YACHT HOTEL
ST. HELIER, JERSEY, C.I.**
TELEPHONE: CENTRAL 1740.

22. The Royal Yacht Hotel facing the bus station, already with its rooftop extension. The early Morris Minor, with split windscreen, confirms that this is a post-war picture, though the awkward-looking roof-top extension went up before the war.

✳

Message on postcard sent to Mrs Smith of Blackpool in 1932:

'Dear Mother
Hope you are having a nice holiday as we are having a good time it is very hot here we are having lovely meals all home grown they have a huge garden with 20 pear trees beside apple trees and even mistletoe.

Love Edith'

✳

Message on postcard sent to Miss J M Woolcock of Bexley, London, in 1936:

'We had a gorgeous day for our crossing, though I did succumb once. The house is in a lovely position, high on a windy hill overlooking St. Aubin's Bay. 9 planes have just arrived on beach below us and returned to England.'

Message on postcard sent to Miss H M Shipway of Southampton in 1936:

'Dear Miss Shipway
Had a good crossing over children very good. Weather is dull but not wet, food is first class so why worry.

Best wishes HM'

✳

British Hotel Jersey.

23. The former British Hotel, on the corner of Bond and Mulcaster Streets, now Barclays Bank.
Postmarked 1908.
(Scottish Photographic Touring & Pictorial Postcard Co. Glasgow)

From an advertisement for St John's Hotel (opposite) in the 1920s.

'Situated in the North of the Island. Only seven minutes walk to Saline Bay, one of the prettiest nooks of the Island. Safe bathing, cabin accommodation, splendid view of Channel Islands and coast of France.'
(La Saline today is a rubbish tip – Ed.)

To Miss V. Crapp of Hounslow, Middlesex:

'Dear Vi,
We are still having a wonderful time and just can't believe the weather. Every day has been hot & sunny. We are sitting here outside a little café overlooking Portelet Sands – you could never imagine such blue sea & sky or such golden sands. Are going to swim again this afternoon – this is the life! Helen very impressed with Jersey. We are going on the island tour next Thursday.

Joan'

24. St. John's Hotel Tea Gardens. This country hotel is situated close to the parish church. Note open-top bullnose Morris emerging from the car park.
(The R.A.P. Co. Ltd., London, E.C.4; Published by F. Salou, Proprietor, St. John's Hotel)

25. St. John's Hotel Recreation Ground. Were we more sporty in the 1920s and '30s? British tennis was certainly more successful than it is today, a fact which perhaps inspired these players.
(The R.A.P. Co. Ltd., London, E.C.4; Published by F. Salou, Proprietor, St. John's Hotel)

Three contrasting interiors...

Message on card postmarked 1910:

'Dear Will & Loo
We are having a grand time here the weather is lovely. I dread coming back to London again. I hope you are all well. I have not heard from anyone at home since I've been here. Love from Lance & your loving sister Esther'

Message to Miss Blundel of Maidstone, Kent, 1937:

'Arrived here Saturday morning feeling like death after a foul trip. Weather not too good so far, hotel quite nice.'

Message on card to Miss P. Ruddick of Mere, Wiltshire, 1953:

'Dear Phylis
We have got some very exciting company on the same table.
                              Best wishes Rita'

26. 14th Century Sitting Room, Finisterre Hotel "Old Smugglers House", Ouaine [sic] Bay. Now no longer an hotel and known simply as 'The Smugglers Inn'. The Finisterre, or 'the end of the world', seems an apt name for this site, leading down to a great sweep of beach, the massive rocks reaching up to Portelet Common and the open sea beyond.
(Albert Smith Ltd., 3 Broad Street, Jersey)

27. Hotel de L'Europe, Jersey; Proprietor P. Trémel. The impressive dining room at this hotel boasted a fine display of palms.

28. The Ship Lounge, Château Rocozanne, St Brelade's Bay, described in an advertisement in 1965 as 'a small, select hotel with the sea at the bottom of the garden'. The modern look, with tubular steel chairs and tables and clean lines everywhere – in sharp contrast to the style of no. 26.

An advertisement for the Aberfeldy from 1955:

'The spacious and delightful lounge is large enough for all requirements. No overcrowding in the busiest times. The five-piece orchestra plays daily in the Dining-room. Dancing nightly in ballroom with frequent Fancy dress and novelty dances.'

※

31. A large gathering of residents at the Aberfeldy, September 6th, 1929. The Aberfeldy, in St. John's Road, was a large establishment which has since been redeveloped as luxury apartments known as Park Heights.
(Albert Smith Ltd., Jersey)

※

Note: Nos. 24 and 25 would have been photographed and made into postcards for sale to the people in the picture.

PARKIN'S HOLIDAY CAMP, PLEMONT, JERSEY. 6840

29. Parkin's Holiday Camp, Plemont. The holiday camp offered a new kind of holiday experience, best suited to families with children. The accommodation was fairly basic, there was plenty of scope for healthy activities and for getting together with fellow holiday-makers. Parkin's, later Pontin's, is now closed and the site, which many say should not have been developed in the first place and should now be left to revert to nature, awaits its fate.
(R.A. [Postcards] Ltd., London, E.C.4)

Parkins Holiday Camp, – from an ad. in 1965:

'The Perfect Holiday on the edge of the Ocean. Brick-built Chalets, Hot & Cold Water, Ballroom, Resident Orchestra, Flood-lit Swimpool, Stage Shows, Tennis Courts, Billiards, Sports and Games, Children's Playground.'

30. A well posed gathering of residents at Swanson's Chelsea House on July 16th, 1929. ("Scotts", Photographers, Jersey)

31.

Message on card postmarked 1947 and sent to Miss Wade of Nottingham:

'Merton Hotel, Jersey

Having a grand time weather and everything ideal. 500 staying at this hotel plenty of life had a lovely crossing should like to stay here.

Love Doris'

From an advertisement from 1937:

'Stands in Own Grounds of 8 acres. Within 2 mins. of Bus and Railway Station, one mile Aerodrome, Sea Bathing from Hotel, Cheerful dining-room, Separate Tables. Own Farm Produce. Near 18-hole Golf Links. Tennis Court. Garage.'

34. Merton Hotel, St. Saviour
Looking more like a block of workers' flats in pre-war Central Europe than a hotel in a holiday isle, the Merton Hotel has a huge capacity. An advertisement from 1955 states that the Merton is the largest hotel in the Channel Islands, accommodating 550 guests.
(Albert Smith Ltd., 3 Broad Street, Jersey)

32. La Falaize, St. Mary's.
The notice overhead states: 'Private Boarding House; Luncheons, Teas & Pic Nic Parties Catered for.'
This card is postmarked 20th July, 1932.
The message reads:

'To-day we came over to Jersey. The picture is the hotel at which we had lunch on our way round the island.'

(A. Laurens Phot., Jersey)

33. Chalet Hotel, Corbière, Jersey. Postmarked 9th August, 1936.

34.

To Mr & Mrs Hayward of Freshwater, Isle of Wight:

'Dear Mum & Dad,

Arrived safely in Jersey after a really wizard journey. Lovely weather on arrival. Passed over IOW. I saw your striped dress.

Love in haste, Bob & Marion'

Message on card postmarked 7 August, 1934, to Mr E Mandy of Cardiff:

'My dear Edwin,

"Sunny" Jersey is not living up to its reputation – rain every day so far. Pity the weather's disappointing – it's a marvellous place. Shall be back on Sunday – if not washed away before then.

Au revoir, B

PS Have gained at least 2 stone'

GROUVILLE HALL HOTEL – JERSEY, C.I.

35. Grouville Hall Hotel
All the cars parked in front are British makes, and note the AA and RAC plaques either side of the entrance porch.
This card is postmarked 24th November, 1958, and sent to Mrs R. of Eastbourne; the message makes interesting reading:

'Well my dear I feel very sad that instead of coming to see you and young Hugh I have had to come here with so little time to spare. It was Hobson's Choice as if I had stayed until I sail for California in January I would have to pay the whole of 1958 income tax which will pay my fare to America. Hope to see you when I get back.'

36. Hautmont Hotel
(Published for Senett & Whinnerah, Photographers, Jersey [by] The R.A. [Postcards] Ltd., London, E.C.4)

37. Plemont Hotel. Postmarked 29th July, 1909.
(Photo, Horace J. Hamon)

36. La Fontaine, Queens Road. Postmarked 14th July, 1954 and addressed to Mr & Mrs Simpson, Lesmahagow, Scotland.
(Speed Publications, Jersey)

37. Pomme D'Or Hotel Gardens
(Albert Smith, Photographer, Jersey)

38. Aerial view of the Demi-Des-Pas Hotel, Havre Des Pas. The hotel has since been demolished and the site redeveloped as apartments.
(No Attribution)

39. Finisterre Hotel, Ouaisné.
(Albert Smith, 3 Broad Street)

Facing St. Catherine's Bay and French Coast.   150 ft. above sea level

LA SOLITUDE FARM,   The only Farm bearing   (MRS.) L. RENOUF,
GOREY, JERSEY.   this name.   Proprietress.
                          Tel. 52 Gorey.

40. Postmarked 27th July, 1903, and addressed to Miss Wise, Hove, Sussex, the message reads as follows:

Arrived here safely. It is an ideal spot. We can look right over to France from our bedroom window. I am writing this by the sea. It is just nice, not too hot. There are 35 people in the house – 2 French families. A good many sleep in a large house on the hill and in some cottages all belonging to the proprietress. I am glad we are in the house – our bedroom is the window next to which I have put a cross. Drawing room underneath. They make up parties for excursions from the house. I think it's going to be very nice

N.

(Albert Smith, Photographer, Jersey)

Getting About

For such a small island, Jersey has a remarkable network of roads – around 600 miles in total. This is partly thanks to General Don, Lieutenant-Governor of Jersey during the Napoleonic Period. Though built originally for military purposes, these highways have been of benefit to locals and tourists alike in their movement around the Island whether travelling by car, bus, motor coach or bicycle.

The advent of rail transport in Jersey came in 1870 with the opening of the line from the Weighbridge in St. Helier to St. Aubin, and its extension, in 1884, to Corbière. The stations in between were as follows: First Tower, Millbrook, Bel Royal, Beaumont, La Haule, St. Aubin, Pont Marquet, Don Bridge, Blanches Banques (for La Moye Golf Links) and La Moye. The Jersey Eastern Railway, opened in 1873, ran from Snow Hill to Gorey via St. Luke's, Grève d'Azette, Samares, Le Hocq, Pontac, La Rocque, Fauvic, Grouville and Gorey Village. At one time it was possible to purchase a through ticket from St. Helier to Paris, via a boat link between Gorey and Carteret in Normandy.

Both lines closed before the war, in 1936 and 1929 respectively. Motor bus services began in 1910 though initially used in conjunction with the railways. For example, to get to Grève de Lecq or Plemont, you would catch the train to Beaumont, then catch the bus. From its peak in the mid-1920s, railway traffic steadily declined in the face of competition from buses and private cars.

Jersey Motor Transport, 'the JMT', and latterly Jersey Bus, provides a comprehensive network of routes to all parts of the island, all routes beginning and ending at the Bus Station in St. Helier. Visitors may also hire cars, scooters and bicycles; the once very popular coach tours are still available, though there are far fewer companies today than during their heyday in the 1950s and '60s.

Message on undated card:

'Dear Mr Leman

The weather has changed over here now, but the first five days were grand. We have been on some lovely coach rides round the island. Beautiful scenery. We really enjoyed ourselves but shall not be sorry to be back in good old England.

Mrs Parkinson'

From Black's Guide to the Channel Islands, 1901:

'A maze of roads and lanes intersect Jersey and Guernsey, sometimes very puzzling, as few have finger-posts. Good inns, many most charmingly situated, are scattered all over Jersey.'

Message on a postcard postmarked 1907:

'Wilfred & I have had a splendid drive this afternoon to the quarries near Devil's Hole, the weather is now splendid although it did not clear until nearly nine o'clock this morning having rained heavily all night.
We have arranged to visit La Rocque on Friday afternoon will probably go by the 2 o'clock Train.'

43. West Park Railway Station with train arriving. This was the first stop on the line west from the Weighbridge to St. Aubin, and later to Corbière. The public conveniences at the entrance to Victoria Park are visible, as is the shelter beside the promenade and, of course, the Grand Hotel and former Bristol Hotel on the corner of Gloucester Street.
(Published by "F.F.", Jersey)

JERSEY-LA HAULE ET CHEMIN DE FER
LA HAULE AND RAILWAY STATION

44. La Haule Railway Station. The first stop after St Aubin on the way back to town. The road is remarkably free of traffic; everyone presumably is in the train which is about to leave. (Published by F.F., Jersey)

Message on card without postmark, presumably sent in an envelope:

'Hotel de France
St. Saviour's Road

I would like to thank you for the arrangements you made to enable my friend & I to have such an enjoyable holiday. Jersey is everything I hoped it would be lovely beaches, a fine shopping centre and a very friendly pleasant hotel. Anybody coming to Hotel de France can be assured of a very enjoyable vacation. The journey over was very rough & my friend was ill but I was able to brave the storm. I do hope you had a good holiday. I am determined to return to Jersey sometime, but would fly next time.

Kind regards
Jean Windsor'

Message on card postmarked 6 July 1928 and sent to E J Cockshott Esq, c/o The Safety Engineer, Post Office Engineering Dept, Bristol:

'at Aberfeldy
St. Heliers

Dear Mr Cockshott,
We are having a glorious holiday. Heaps of sunshine, sometime 14-15 hrs a day. Am almost a Red Indian. Expect to come back thoroughly fit & help shove things along.

KR'
[signature illegible]

44. Pontac Railway Station on the East Coast line. Postmarked 17th April, 1908, and addressed to Madamoiselle Lemoigne, Directrice de l'école publique, Coutances, France. The message reads:

'Bons Souvenirs et bons baisons.
L Dupleme'

(P.C. by J Welch & Sons, Portsmouth. Printed at our Works in Belgium)

47. Train at Gorey Station, terminus on the East Coast line. This card is postmarked 10th August, 1902, the year in which it was first permitted for correspondents to include their message on the card's address side. The sender in this case confined her message to the illustration:

I wish you were here. We are having a lovely time. There are heaps of nice people here. Are you away on your holidays. We shall not be home for a month yet. Write if you have time. Be good.
Best love, Maude.

Addressed to Miss Hilda Foulkes, Southport, Lancashire

(Raphael Tuck & Sons' "County" Postcard No. 3203. Phototyped in Berlin)

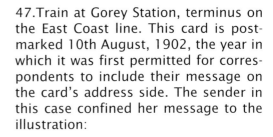

45.

46. Gorey Village Station, Jersey Eastern Railway
(F. Foot)

47.

49. Sent to Mrs Heaps of Leeds:

'Ask Madge if she can find Daddy. Hope you are well, beautiful weather here & a lovely island will be leaving here on Saturday night all being well, hope to be home on Monday.   EH'

(Albert Smith, Photographer, Jersey)

'Harry, the well known guide of Jersey' Harry is one in a long tradition of people who have made their living by acting as guides to holidaymakers.
(Cecil de Beer, Jersey)

50. This card is postmarked 25th September, 1915, and addressed to Mrs Dumbleton in Brighton.
The message reads:

'Dear Ma
What do you think of this taken of our party yesterday at Prince's Tower, the highest point in the Island. The lady with the white hat in the break & I constitute the Poly. party. Don't you think this rather good of Sonny [the heavily whiskered man in the centre].
                    Love from George'

(Albert Smith, Jersey)

48. A well laden horse-drawn carriage. Like the hotel group photographs (nos. 30 & 31), these pictures of holidaymakers about to set off (probably on a tour of the island) were taken to be offered for sale to the individuals depicted. (A. Laurens)

49. *From a Guide Book published in 1902:*

'There are several livery stables each have their own stereotyped rounds, which are announced in the hotels the night before. Fare 2s.6d. a head. The cars call at the hotels, and at lodgings if required. A tip for the guide, whose information must not always be trusted.'

50.

51. From horse-drawn carriages to motor-driven charabancs. The more modern attire of the holidaymakers suggests that this picture was taken after the First World War. Indeed, the card is postmarked 4th September, 1919. Addressed to Mr & Mrs Ford of Sherborne, Dorset, the message reads:

'Dear Papa & Blanche,
Just a line to let you know all's well. Have had a good time here and feel much better. Returning to Dorchester by Saturday's boat. The crossings have been pretty rough lately.
Love Charlie'

(Albert Smith, Jersey)

Message to Mr Pipe of Hornsey, London, 1913:

'We had a very rough crossing coming over and I got a nasty cut on the leg, but we are doing alright now.
Fred'

52. A jolly sunlit party photographed at Portelet on July 10th. We don't know which year, but the vehicle is a good deal less antiquated than that in no. 51. An impressive display of frilly sun hats though the gentleman third left at the back has stuck to the traditional knotted hanky.
("Scotts", Photographers, Jersey)

53. Horse-drawn taxi cabs awaiting fares at Queens Gardens. Note the hotels opposite: the Great Western Hotel, left (now 'The Bridge' pub) and the L & S W Hotel, centre – the two rival railway companies which operated passenger boats to and from Jersey.
(Trichromatic P.C. by J Welch & Sons, Portsmouth. Printed at our Works in Belgium)

51.

52.

53.

54. Weighbridge, St. Helier, showing J.M.T. (Jersey Motor Transport) buses assembled, including double-deckers. Motor taxis are lined up on the far side. Also note the potato lorries queueing for the Weighbridge. Queens Gardens were eventually cleared to allow the expansion of the Bus Station.

This card is postmarked 5th June, 1954, and is addressed to Mr Shergold of Southsea, Hampshire. The message reads:

Dear Pop. Writing this high up the cliffs looking out to Bouley Bay. It's a wee bit warmer today – but we still are wearing our top coats – no sign of sun. The cross on the front marks the Hotel where we are staying [The Pomme D'Or]. Glad you went to the pictures & you are OK. Sorry to hear about Mr Wilkins – he hadn't looked strong to me for a while now. Give my Babe a pat. What size collar does she take? Please.

Love, Irene XX

(Valentine & Sons Ltd., Dundee and London)

St. Helier

'A Large Harbour; a maze of streets, busy and prosperous, but noted for their cleanliness; a huge fort rising perpendicularly above the town; good shops; numerous places of worship; a miscellaneous assortment of carriages and well-appointed "Jersey cars", plus a general air of comfort and well-being, are the prominent features of St. Helier.' This was the description of town from a guide book published between the wars.

St. Helier was the place where many visitors stayed, in hotels or boarding houses. Even if they did not stay in town, it was where most of them did their shopping before returning home. Today most of the shops are, regrettably, the same shops in any High Street on the mainland, though a few of the largest are still Jersey concerns and retain their individual character. In the 1920s, Voisin's of King Street advertised themselves as 'General Drapers, Outfitters, Complete House Furnishers and Confectioners.'

De Gruchy's, just yards away, was 'The Oldest and Largest Drapery Establishment in the Channel Islands; Established 1810', and are 'General Drapers and House Furnishers, High-Class Tailors and Outfitters, Hosiers, Hatters, etc., Milliners, Dressmakers and Ladies' Tailors.'

Owing to Jersey's tax-free status, visitors were tempted to buy goods which were more expensive on the mainland. These included perfumes; Jersey Eau de Cologne was manufactured and sold by Larbalestier, Luce, Dubras and De Faye (by Royal Appointment). Alcohol and tobacco were the other main staples of the duty-free trade. The local cigarette company, Ching & Co., promised that their Navy Cut Cigarettes 'will add the last touch of enjoyment to your Holidays'; they were 6d. a pack of 20 before the war.

Aside from shopping opportunities, 'In addition to its convenience as a centre, the town is lively with evening entertainments.'

59 JERSEY. — *St. Hélier.* - *Place du Poids Public.*
The Weigh-Bridge. — LL.

55.

16-17/9/03.

The Parliament House & Royal Square Jersey.

JW&S 434

56.

55. The Weighbridge
Postmarked 24th July, 1909,
sent by Suzanne Gérard and
addressed to Madame Genet,
Boulogne, France. This
Edwardian view shows streets
free of traffic save for a few
taxi-cabs awaiting fares beside
Queen's Gardens. The
Southampton and Royal Yacht
Club Hotels are still pretty
much intact today but
compare the original roofline
of the Royal Yacht to that
depicted about 50 years later
in no.20.
(L L)

56. The Parliament House and
Royal Square
Dated 1903; the horse chestnut
trees were planted in 1894,
hence their small stature. The
Parliament House is more
usually known as the States
Chambers. Formerly the Market
Square, and the central public
space where the Battle of Jersey
was won in 1781 and where
important pronouncements are
made, the Royal Square can fairly be
described as the heart of St Helier and,
therefore, the heart of the island. The
tower of the Town Church can be seen
in the middle distance. The statue of
King George II, masquerading as a
Roman Emperor, originally erected in
1751, has witnessed many changes over
the past two and a half centuries; his
presence there gave rise to the local
saying, 'There's only one good man in
Jersey and he's in the Royal Square.'
Notice how all the figures are standing
still while the photographer takes his
picture.
(JW&S 434)

57. Public Library, Royal Square. This
more detailed view shows this fine
building to advantage. Opened in
1886, the Bibliotheque served the
public until 1989, when the new
library opened in Halkett Place.
(Pitt Series No. 24; Photo F. Foot)

53 JERSE

Three views of King Street...

58. No postmark date but most probably sometime between the wars. This is at the junction with Halkett Place. Sent to a Mrs Robertson of Edinburgh, the message reads:

'This place is by no means a one horse town, it has its traffic problems as well as any other although to look at the policemen and the helmets they wear you'd think you were in India.
                                    Albert'

(No attribution but 'A Real Bromide Photograph; British Manufacture')

✳

59. Junction with Halkett Place

KING STREET, JERSEY.

59.

54

60. Junction with Halkett Place
(J. Welch & Sons, Portsmouth)

61. King Street
(LL ; Printed in France)

Church and Chapel...

62. Parish Church, St. Helier.

63. All Saints Church in The Parade. Apart from the loss of some of the trees in the Great Hurricane of 1987, this scene has not changed. In particular, the solid granite bollards are still intact, if a little distressed in places. (Pitt series no. 24)

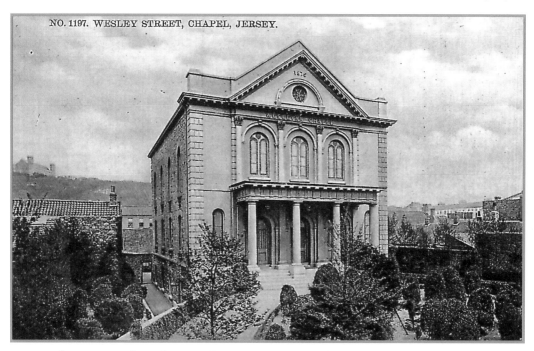

64. Wesley Street Chapel, St. Helier. (Godfray, Jersey)

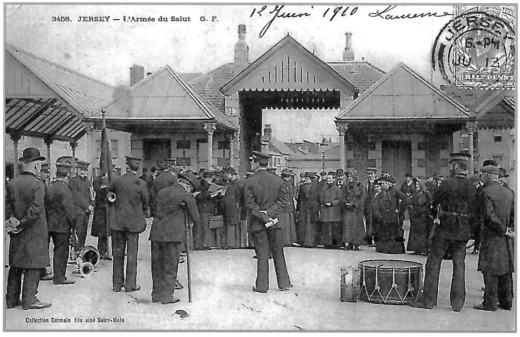

65. Salvation Army at The Weighbridge. Posted in 1910 to Monsieur Boyer in Paris. The French seem to have held a fascination with the Salvation Army, as the many French-produced postcards testify.(Collection Germain fils aîné Saint-Malo)

82 JERSEY. - St-Hélier - L'Église Catholique. - Catholic Church. - L.

66. St. Thomas' Catholic Church, also known as 'the French Cathedral' viewed from Victoria Street. This picture must have been taken quite soon after it opened in 1887.
(L.L. Printed in France)

Post-war shopping street scenes...

Message on postcard sent in 1948, a time of strict rationing on the mainland:

From a booklet on Jersey published by the Jersey Chamber of Commerce, 1955:

'The Grand
Spending 14 days here. A very fine Island for a holiday. Lots of stock in shops at reasonable prices. No tax. Want of coupons keeps purchases down to minimum.'

'The town of St. Helier, capital of the Island, still retains much of a Continental atmosphere and has numerous features of charm and interest. There are many fine shops, ancient markets and a characteristic gaiety and brightness of special appeal to visitors.'

67. Queen Street. Boots can be seen in the middle distance. Postmarked 20th July, 1953, and addressed to Mrs Milner of Chigwell, Essex, the message reads:

'Dear Phyl,
Hope you have nice weather when you go on your holiday. I would like it better if not so many hills. We both took poor view of the plane flight.
                                    Love Gert'

(R.A. [Postcards] Ltd., London, E.C.4)

68. Broad Street. Looking towards Charing Cross. The main Post Office is on the left.
(R.A. [Postcards] Ltd., London, E.C.4)

69. Charing Cross. There are many changes of detail in this scene today, notably the 1970s' pedestrianisation of King Street, but it is still easily recognisable.
(Salmon Series)

From a Jersey guide book in 1965:
'Wherever you go to do your shopping, you may be sure of a very real welcome and the courtesy and helpfulness for which Jersey is renowned.'

✳

Message on card sent to E L Nicholls of Portsmouth:

'Parkins Holiday Camp
Plemont

Dear Mum
Arrived after exciting journey saw fire near Southampton, stopped by fog & arrived 4.45 in morning but had breakfast on board and left at 6.30. Having grand time. Everything cheap even bought you a bottle of Eau de Cologne for £7.11.2d what is 15s there. Coming home Sunday morning.   Keith'

Message on card sent to Miss Emery of Bromley, Kent:

'Dear Sylvia,

Just a note to say I arrived alright, just in time for lunch! – at 12.20 to be precise. The weather is much too good to be true but here's hoping that it stays the way it is now – or possibly a little <u>cooler</u>. It seems as if I am staying at one of the best places in town – so I should do alright – especially with cigarettes at 1/6 for 20. What I have seen of the scenery seems to be worth looking at & there are no crowds, even in St. Helier on a Saturday!

Love Ted'

✳

Edwardian Street Scenes...

70. Midvale Road. Postmarked September 7th, 1909, this view is from the junction with Val Plaisant with the spire of what is now St. Columba's Church of Scotland in the middle distance.

74 — Jersey - St Helier — David place

71. David Place. Dated 30th July, 1906 and addressed to Mme. Fournetmère of Paris. Looking north with spire of St. Mark's Church in distance.

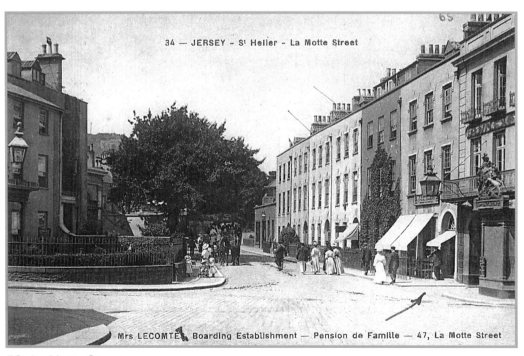

34 — JERSEY - St Helier - La Motte Street

Mrs LECOMTE, Boarding Establishment — Pension de Famille — 47, La Motte Street

72. La Motte Street.

Message on card sent to Mr & Mrs B of Burnham on Sea, postmarked 9 August, 1960:

'We had a lovely journey over, no one was ill, there were over a thousand on board, we arrived at 6. We have good digs, right in the centre of town, it is a bit noisy at night, ever such a large town it has been very hot, getting browned off.

Cheerio, Alf & Ethel'

Message on card sent to Mrs S of Malmesbury, postmarked 19 June, 1955:

'Having a good time here. Very warm with lots of sunshine. Have been in the sea & in the pubs. Am now like a red indian.

Cheers, Mabel'

Message on card sent to Mrs Cox of Sheffield, postmarked 12 July, 1938:

'Aberfeldy, Jersey
Dear Mum & Dad
Weather here simply terrible – very cold & wet. No sun since Friday. We can't even get English newspapers while the weather is so bad.

Love Gladys'

Message on card sent to Miss W of Exeter, postmarked 22 May, 1953:

'Ommaroo Hotel
We are very happy & comfortable & well-fed here, making plans to cover as much as possible of the Island. I enjoyed the flight very much indeed & could hardly believe what was happening to me.

Yours, M.K. Stokes'

73. John W. Orviss. These impressive retail premises were on the corner of Beresford and Halkett Streets. Orviss was where shoppers went for the best groceries and provisions. This later became a Le Riche supermarket until its move to the ground floor of Le Gallais in Bath Street.

Market Fountain in Winter, Jersey.

75. The Market. At the junction of Beresford Street and Halkett Place. Postmarked July 26th, 1904, 22 years after the Market was opened. It remains one of the great buildings of St. Helier.

Addressed to Miss Thomas of Hastings, the message reads simply:

'Do you remember this?

Lulu'

76. Looking down on market stalls – Huelin Renouf in evidence. Note gas lighting. Postmarked September 22nd, 1912, addressed to Miss Godden of Reading:

'Dear Miss G
Still having quite a nice time, the weather is now perfect. I shall soon have to be thinking of returning...
Yours very sincerely

Lily Ellis'

74. Market fountain in winter. I wonder how many times this has happened since the market opened? Postmarked February 25th, 1904, and addressed to Mr Huelin in Dartford, Kent
(Albert Smith, photo, Jersey)

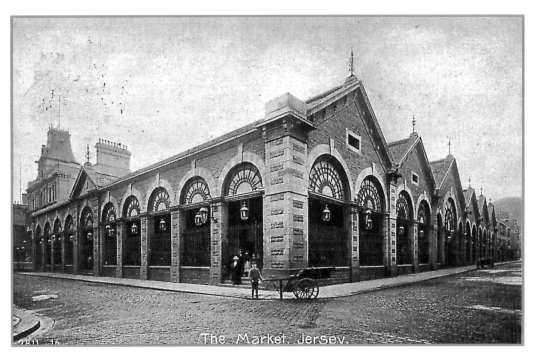

75.

76.

Three views in The Parade Gardens...

Jersey - The Parade

77. The diagonal path looking towards the junction of The Parade and Elizabeth Place, with the bust of P. Baudains, Constable of St. Helier for 15 years, in the centre. The Parade, once well wooded – see also no. 78 – lost many of its trees in the Great Hurricane of 1987. Postmarked 23rd May, 1904, and addressed to Monsieur Louis de Buzonnière in Orléans, France. The card also bears the stamp of 'Hotel de la Pomme D'Or'. (The "Beresford" Series)

Message on card sent to Mr & Mrs Hawkins of Walsall:

'Dear Mother,
Just to let you know we arrived safely late on Saturday night after a nightmare journey – never come to Jersey unless by air! The hotel is very good but conditions generally are poor. Food very expensive indeed compared to n/c. Only things very cheap are make-up, perfume and high class leather goods. It is a smokers paradise – will bring some back for Dad. Bought a camera today so will have some snaps to show you
Love Eileen'

Message on card sent to Mrs & Miss N. of Norwich, postmarked 7 August, 1954:

'We are thoroughly enjoying our stay in Jersey. It is very pretty and the various bays so different from each other. The town is so packed with people but it is still possible to get away & find a quiet beach. Today it is very wild & we do wish the weather would become more settled.

W.W.R.'

78. The Parade Gardens. View from the junction of The Parade and Gloucester Street. The Don Monument is clearly visible in the distance. Undated and no postmark but, judging by the fashions, this view is probably of the Edwardian period. (G.F.)

79. A similar view to no. 78, but some 50 years later, showing the Cenotaph. A Tantivy Motors signboard can be seen on the left and a banner advertising 'Salads & Vegetarian Dishes'. (R.A. [Postcards] Ltd., London, E.C.4)

80. Triangle Park. The bandstand stood where the statue of Queen Victoria now stands. The former name of this open space owes its origin to its shape, wedged as it is between Pierson Road, St. Aubin's Road and The Esplanade. It is now known as Victoria Park.

81. West Park Avenue. This street of solidly built and rather ornate Victorian town houses survives largely unchanged. (Pitt Series No. 37)

82. Elizabeth Place. Parade Gardens on the right.
(Photo F.Foot)

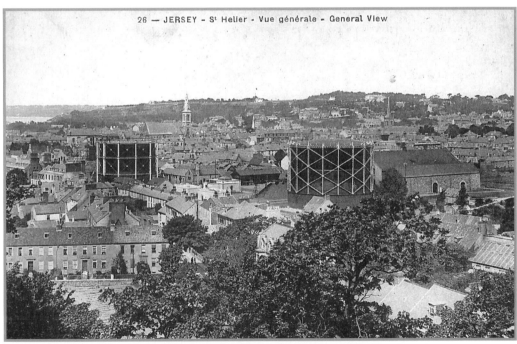

26 — JERSEY - St Helier - Vue générale - General View

83. St. Helier from Victoria College with gas holders and church spires.

Message sent to Mr J Nowell of Balham, London, in 1950:

'Dear Jeffery

Here is a pleasant view of one of the bays. I've toured most of the Island by cycle, using a map of pubs! The French wines are extremely palatable.

See you soon, Sid'

Message sent to Mrs Walters of Cardiff in 1910:

'Dear Mother

It is real hot here to-day. I shall have to buy some new white pants. Every one goes in for bathing here although it is not so pleasant for it as the Isle of Wight. The tide goes out very far here.

With love from Alan'

From a booklet on Jersey published by the Jersey Chamber of Commerce, 1955:

'A delightful retreat is found in Howard Davis Park. These beautifully kept grounds, with their trim lawns and well-stocked flower beds, lie on the outskirts of the town of St. Helier. Band Concerts and other entertainments are held in the Park during the Summer Season.'

Message to P J Knowles of Kingsteignton, Devon, in 1906:

'Dear Puss,

You ought to spend a holiday here to improve your French. The French we spoke (!) before coming was all wrong, but we are quite fluent now.'

83. St. Luke's District. View from Mount Bingham. This part of town, then not completely built up, takes its name after St. Luke's Church.

84. Howard Davis Park was one of many gifts to the island by T.B. Davis, a Jerseyman who made a fortune in shipping in South Africa, in memory of his son Howard who was killed in the First World War.
(M and L National Series))

85. Howard Davis Park.
(Valentine & Sons Ltd., Dundee and London)

87. Pierson Road. View south along Pierson Road with the apex of Triangle Park in the middle foreground. Pierson Road is built up on the east side and faces the park. It consists an attractive range of Victorian houses, happily still largely intact today. Apart, that is, from the pointed roof on the tower to the left. This was formerly known as the Cannon Tower Hotel but was rechristened the Town Park Hotel when the tower lost its roof. Sadly, the Town Park opened its doors to guests for the last time in 2001.

Message on a card postmarked 27th June, 1956, addressed to Miss Pascoe of Bideford, Devon:

'We certainly are lucky with the weather. Wilson says he's only coming back to earn enough money to come to Jersey again. It's an ideal spot. Went to a French revue Monday evening which was very good indeed. See you Friday when we come to earth with a bang.

Love W & Y'

St. Helier-by-sea

One of the features which holiday-makers looked for in a coastal resort was the opportunity for casual strolling along the front, in the vicinity of the beach and sea. St. Helier offered this in abundance. On the west side of town was The Esplanade, where folk could wander from the Weighbridge to West Park and beyond. And they could venture over the causeway to Elizabeth Castle – more of an adventure before the reclamation of the beach west of Albert Pier.

Old guide books extol the attractions of 'West End Bathing Pool', or 'Victoria Marine Lake', as it was sometimes referred to. This opened in 1897: 'There is every convenience for both swimmers and non-swimmers – rafts, spring boards and double diving stage (5 feet and 9 feet high). A boatman is always in attendance.'

The Esplanade was a great place to take the air but 'unfortunately, so severe are the south-west gales during winter that it has proved impossible to get young trees to withstand their devastating effects, and the promenade has consequently a rather bare appearance.'

Most nineteenth century expansion of St. Helier took place in a northerly direction; the St. Luke's area to the east of Fort Regent was not fully developed until the first quarter of the twentieth century, although the shoreline at Havre des Pas had been an important area for shipbuilding in the 1800s.

As the tourism industry developed, more hotels and boarding houses opened in this area and the promenade at La Collette, with its incomparable gardens, were created.

The present reclamation of the shore at La Collette will change forever the aspect for promenaders here but there remains the enjoyable stroll along the front past the slipway by Hotel de la Plage and the wonderfully curved sea wall before reaching the recently restored Bathing Pool at Havre des Pas (first opened 1895) and on to the Dicq.

Four views of The Esplanade at West Park, or West End, as it was once known...

88. View taken from Mont Patibulaire (otherwise known as West Mount), looking towards the Esplanade at West Park. The most prominent building, apart from the Grand Hotel, is the Opera House. (L.L.)

89. Looking east. Note the Bristol Hotel and the railed enclosure for the railway track. (L.L.)

*137. - Jersey. - St-HELIER
Sur la plage à marée haute. - On the Beach. - E. L.*

90. Looking west. Note the stripy bathing huts, which bathers used for changing, on the slipway and the railing along its right-hand side. The single-storey building on the right was a military picket house, used when a detachment of soldiers was stationed at Elizabeth Castle. (E.L. Printed in France)

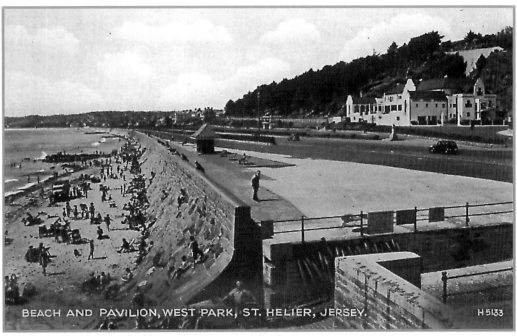

BEACH AND PAVILION, WEST PARK, ST. HELIER, JERSEY.   H 5133

91. Beach and West Park Pavilion. post-1931. (Valentine)

92.

WEST PARK SANDS AND POOL, JERSEY.

93.

92. 'On the Sand at Jersey'
A crowded beach at West Park. Mostly children and a few mothers, all behatted and well clothed.
(The F.F. Phototone Series)

✳

93. 'West Park Sands and Pool'
A similar view as no. 92 but from the sea wall, most likely taken between the wars. The flag near the centre denotes the Daily Mail Sand Castle Building Competition, the sort of organised fun which would be unusual today.

✳

94. Elizabeth Castle
An evocative moonlit view from West Mount across Victoria Avenue and the bathing pool.

✳

95. Great Electric Storm, Aug. 28, 1931. (Albert Smith Ltd., Jersey)

Elizabeth Castle, Jersey.

94.

Great Electric Storm, Jersey Aug 28 1931.

95.

ELIZABETH CASTLE. JERSEY.

96. A solitary figure returning along the causeway from Elizabeth Castle, a trek which thousands of Jersey visitors have made.
(The "FF. Chromotint Series")

1129 ELIZABETH CASTLE, JERSEY.

97. A view of Elizabeth Castle across the sea.
(Godfray's Series. Jersey '07)

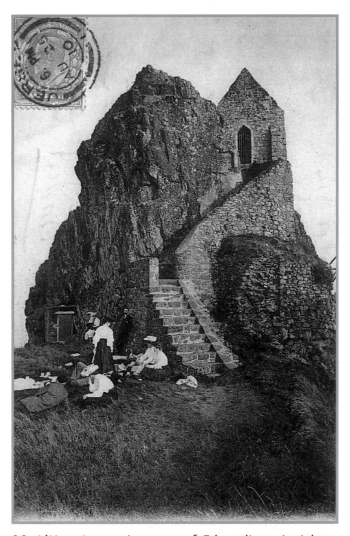

98. L'Hermitage. A group of Edwardian picnickers beneath St. Helier's Hermitage. Postmarked August 25th, 1910, addressed to Mr Simonet in Paris.
(L.L. Printed in France)

Three views of La Collette, the other side of St Helier...

Message to Miss Joan Slade of Orpington (undated):

'Dear Joan,

I am enjoying myself very much here but my parents don't like the 'atmosphere' much. I won the mixed doubles table tennis last week. I'll be bringing some photos taken at dances.

Jeff'

From Ward Lock's Guide, 1937:
'From the south end of Pier Road a path winds round the stunted tower called La Collette, near which is the Men's Bathing Station (free). At high tide the bathers enter the water from a wooden pier; at low water from specially prepared diving places among the rocks, to which access is gained by cement paths. There are no cabins here; bathers must undress among the rocks.'

LA COLLETTE, JERSEY.

98. Postmarked 23rd August, 1932. A view eastwards featuring the diving stage of the Jersey Swimming Club.
("Pelham" Post Card)

100. La Collette Gardens. Dated 1950.
(English Series Post Card: Photographed, Printed and Published by Photo-Precision Ltd., St. Alban's)

100. La Collette Gardens

Another three views of La Collette...

LA COLLETTE WALK, JERSEY.

102. A sunny view westwards taken from near the slipway which is the meeting point of La Collette and Havre des Pas.

Message on card posted in 1946:

Dear All

You would all love a holiday here if you came by air as I did. It was a glorious trip of 1 hr 40 mins from Croydon. Jersey is very nice & the little bays all round the island are really beautiful & quiet. The weather has been simply glorious & we are enjoying every moment of our stay here. Milk is not rationed & wherever you go you see people buying glasses of milk just as you do ice cream. In the hotel at lunch times it is strange to see grown up people all ordering glasses of milk with their lunch. Hotel is also licensed.

Fred

A visitor from Guernsey in 1934 wrote home:

We had a most glorious crossing & Mum wasn't ill at all. The traffic here is awful, much worse than Guernsey.

Message to Mrs J. of Erdington, Birmingham, in 1957:

'Having rather nice weather at present with plenty to eat and being waited on at the hotel by French waiters.

From Mrs Green'

103. View looking west along La Collette from the Green Street slipway, with small girls. Probably 1920s.
(F.F., Jersey)

104. Looking east from La Collette, beyond the Green Street slipway, towards Havre des Pas. Note the hoarding where Hotel de la Plage now stands.
(Pitt Series No, 79)

Three views of Havre-des-Pas...

105. View along the beach towards the Dicq, probably pre-First World War – plenty of straw hats in evidence.
(Pitt Series No. 80)

106. The Red Mine at Havre-Des-Pas
Postmarked 22nd September, 1956
(R.A. (Postcards) Ltd. London, E.C.4)

From Ward Lock's Guide, 1937:
'A promenade, substantially built of granite and cement, with seats every few yards, leads from La Collette to the Havre des Pas Esplanade, and at its eastern end passes several cafés, some in the open air – a little group that reminds one very strongly of Continental resorts, especially in the evening.'

108. Fort d'Auvergne Hotel, Havre-Des-Pas.
Note the lettering and arrow on left-hand side indicating 'Exit to Sunbathing Beach'.
Postmarked 29 July 1954, addressed to Miss G of Newport in the Isle of Wight:

'My dear Susan,

Thought you might like this picture of our Hotel here, the window fourth from the left as you look at the card is our bedroom. No rain this week, but such a terrible high wind it nearly blows us away. Looking forward to the Battle of Flowers. See you soon. Love to all.

Auntie & Uncle'

105.

THE RED MINE at HAVRE-DES-PAS, JER...

106.

107. Group photograph taken by itinerant photographer and printed by "HAPPY SNAPS" of Broad Street. The owner noted the date 1936 and the names, from l to r.: 'Self, Bert, Dick, Edie, Frank.' (Reduced from postcard-size)

108.

Havre des Pas Bathing Pool...

109. The fun people had before Health and Safety rules and regulations put an end to diving boards!
Postmarked 25th August, 1932, addressed to Miss Collins of Teignmouth, Devon:

'This is a marvellous place – weather brilliant but not too overpowering. Hotel seems fairly normal tho' some of the people rather mad. Food good tell your mother. Have done a trip to Grève de Lecq and one round the island – marvellous bathing beaches. Two rather nice fellows here, met them out to sea – went to West Park Pavilion dancing with them.
Love Hilda'

(J.R.Rowland, Jersey)

From Ward Lock Guide, 1937:
'The pool is roughly horse-shoe shaped: its walls encloses as area of over 2 acres. At the shallow end is a special place for beginners and non-swimmers. The depth increases to 12 feet under the high diving stage.
Spring boards and fixed boards are provided for divers, and there is a long water chute. There are swimming courses of 110 and 50 yards, over which a national championship is generally held once a year. In addition, various swimming galas take place from time to time. One of the most exciting events is the annual swimming match between Jersey and Guernsey when some excellent racing is seen, as the two islands are very keen rivals. Overlooking the shallow end of the pool is a terrace where sun-bathing can be enjoyed at leisure and where refreshments may be obtained. On Tuesday and Friday evenings this terrace is the scene of open-air dancing.'

HAVRE-DES-PAS BATHING POOL, JERSEY. G.2107

109.

110. Note mispelling of 'Havre'. Probably 1930s.
(Valentine & Sons, Ltd., Dundee and London)

111. Probably 1950s or '60s.
(Published by B.B. London)

112. Captioned 'La Collette', but more accurately Havre-des-Pas, looking east from the junction with Roseville Street. The former footbridge to the Bathing Pool is on the left. Probably 1920s.

Message on card sent to Mr & Mrs M. of Bedford in 1952:

'Arrived OK. This is a really lovely island. Weather scorching hot. We shall soon look like cooked lobsters. Smashing Hotel – waiters are all Italian – good food. Things here are dirt cheap – beer 6d a pint – cigarettes 20 for 1/6d. The scenery here is absolutely marvellous – are having a really lovely time.

Love to you all. Pip & Geoff'

A Trip around the Island

A small island with such varied scenery demanded to be seen, and the means of doing so has developed over the years of tourism in Jersey.

A hundred years ago, visitors toured in horse-drawn carriages, known as excursion-cars: 'During the summer, excursion cars leave St. Helier several times daily for all parts of the Island, and are largely patronised. Each car has a conductor who points out objects of interest, *en route*, and endeavours to be of use to everybody, even to the extent of obliging with songs and music.'

Two prominent livery stables were Down's in David Place and the Paragon in Grove Place. Horse-drawn excursion cars were followed in the 1920s by motor charabancs, then by motor coaches: 'During the summer it is possible to visit almost every beauty spot in the island by motor-coach. The majority of these vehicles start from the open space at the Weighbridge. There are daily trips around the Island, leaving between 10 and 11am and returning in time for dinner, while shorter afternoon and evening trips specialize in particular localities. The fares are usually about 5s. for a day trip, 2s.6d. afternoon, and 2s. evening.' This advice was published in a guide book in 1937. The prices remained much the same throughout the 1950s.

There were always alternatives to the organised coach tour – Edwardian visitors loved to walk, often availing themselves of the train to reach starting points or to return to town. Many visitors brought their bicycles with them or hired machines once in the island. And latterly, of course, many visitors hire cars to get around the Island.

The postcard views that follow are arranged in an anti-clockwise direction, which is how I remember the Round the Island coach tour in the 1950s.

Journey to the south-east corner of the island...

Message to Mr & Mrs Peel of Helenborough, Scotland, 1951:

> This is an ideal place for a holiday. Continual sunshine, lovely beaches, 1st class Hotel & French cooking – we <u>must all</u> come here.

✳

An anonymous message to Miss Brown of Chiswick, London, 1949:

> 'We have had a most perfect week, but a week does not really warrant the journey. We have completely toured the coast of the island. Everything brown instead of green under the very hot sun and nearly all the inhabitants speaking French (a patois thereof) amongst themselves.

Message on card sent in 1929:

> Dear Eva
>
> Here are the three lost souls gazing at the mud or sea having just passed this Castle on a 2/6 tour. We had a fairly good crossing. The hotel is quite nice; the weather lovely: so all is well. Best love from your big daughter and the rest of the noisy crowd.
>
> Love Ida, Annie and Gertie XXXXXX

✳

113. Le Hocq Tower

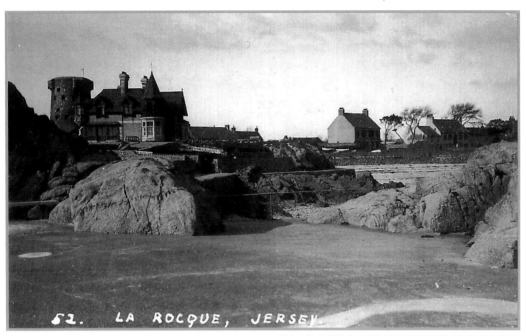

114. Sent 10th October 1935 to Mrs Tothill of Perth, Western Australia:

'I had a lovely picnic given me at this place "La Rocque" Jersey.
The beaches are beautiful.'

115. La Rocque Harbour (Regatta Day).
(Pitt Series No. 87)

Approaching Gorey, bastion of the east coast...

116. View from the sea wall at high tide. The promenade is well protected from both the sea and the railway track.
(Lévy et Neurdein Réunis, 44, Rue Letellier, Paris. Printed in France)

※

Message from a card sent in 1935, to Miss Boulton of Oxford:

'I'm having a lovely time over here, it's a beautiful place, & so much to see. Cigarettes 20 for 4d, beer 4d pint, in fact we just LIVE. Weather is hot & I'm bathing every day. Kindest regards.

E. Rowlands.'

※

118. To Mrs J Hawkins of Hammersmith, London:

'This will be the last card from Jersey – yesterday was lovely, today pouring again – but we have just got to accepting it now. Think we have put on weight.

Eileen'

(Phototype" postcard. Valentine & Sons, Ltd., Dundee and London)

Message to Miss Gosset of Liphook, Hampshire, 1947:

'Jersey is lovely though the crossing was foul. I succumbed to the movement of the waves.'

116.

117. View from Gorey Hill showing the Castle, the railway track and station and Gorey Hill.

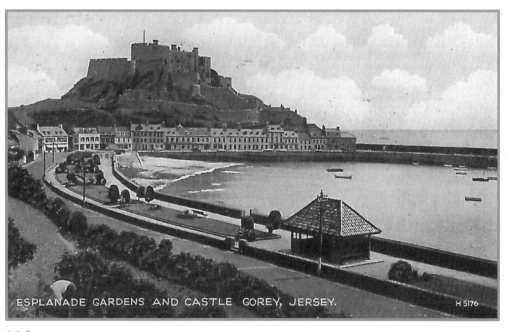

ESPLANADE GARDENS AND CASTLE GOREY, JERSEY.   H 5176

118.

119. Mont Orgueil Castle. Postmarked 21 August, 1951, sent to Mr & Mrs Clark of Rottingdean, Sussex:

'Still enjoying life here. All looking like niggers. Feel I could stay another week, but all good things come to an end. All the best to all, Dollie'

(R.A. [Postcards] Ltd., London EC4)

※

120. A nicely composed picture of the attractive sweep of buildings lining Gorey Pier with the shapely bulk of Mont Orgueil Castle looming beyond.
(Speed Publication, Jersey)

※

121. Sailing ships moored at Gorey. Postmarked March 4th, 1912, addressed to Miss Simpson of Edinburgh:

'Am seeing as much of the island as I can. Going to see Corbière lighthouse this afternoon. A very wild part there. Having a good time & sorry to leave so soon.   Love Fred'

(Peacock Series)

※

Message to Miss Ashworth of Rochdale, 1926:

'Jersey is a wonderful place – everything is of such a vivid colour, rocks, sea, sky & vegetation is like none I have ever seen – everything seems huge compared to things at home.'

MONT ORGUEIL CASTLE (FLOODLIT) GOREY, JERSEY.   12265

119.

120.

121.

CAFÉ CAPRI, GOREY. JERSEY.   No 1

122. Café Capri, Gorey. Postmarked 23rd August, 1954 and addressed to Mrs Gowers of Godalming, Surrey:

(A.G.L.M. Jersey)

'Dear Mum & Dad,
It's a lovely day today, at least up to so far, we are going to make it a lazy one too, we are having morning coffee here.'

Hillcrest Cafe
GOREY. JERSEY C.1.

123. Hillcrest Café, Gorey.

Message to Mrs Shotton of Consett, Co. Durham:

'I am having a wonderful time here. This is a perfect place for the holiday. The island is so beautiful and the weather so good. Consett seems very far away.'

'Dear Mum
Please send us a parcel of good weather, we're having rain & winds so far, nevertheless we are enjoying ourselves.'

Message on card postmarked 25 July, 1931, to Miss C Berry of Lyme Regis, Dorset:

'I hope your spots have gone and that you are feeling quite OK. I walked seven miles to see this Castle! The weather is glorious but my arms are blistered with the sun
                        Love from Nurse'

Message on card sent to Mrs Pybus of Stockton-on-Tees in 1947:

'Dear Marm
Weather and eats are grand. Everyone feasting their faces and lying in the sun and haunting the shops.'

124. Mont Orgueil Castle & Tea Houses (J. Welch & Sons, Portsmouth)

Message on card sent in 1954 to Mr & Mrs Fenwick of Wembley, Middlesex:

'Having a very happy time. Weather just to our liking. Both enjoyed plane journey & have finished coming by sea as saving of time makes such a difference. We are both feeling very refreshed and well. This time next week back to usual routine. We leave Thurs 3.15. I think one pint of milk & a small loaf will do.'

Message from card sent to Mr G. Wynn of Sheppereton, Middlesex in 1958:

'Dear Nobby,
Having a very nice time here with bags of talent about but most of it's sixteen or sixty. They've got scooters here but they keep braking (sic) down. Having a good old session every night & what with that and swimming every day I feel just about clapped out.

Brian'

To Mr Wetherill of High Wycombe, 1952:

'Dear Mum & Dad
What tobacco do you want?
Reply all speed.

Norman'

To Miss Stanpool of Stockbridge, 1946:

'Had a lovely day on a farm yesterday, plenty to eat, the bread and cakes are much nicer than ours.

Love Lillian'

125. Anne Port, looking south.

ARCHIRONDELLE TOWER & St CATHERINE'S BAY, JERSEY.   R.331.

126. Archirondel Tower & St. Catherine's Bay.
(The "Dainty" Series)

63. JERSEY. — St Catherine's Bay

H. G. Allix, édit., Jersey

127. St. Catherine's Bay. Postmarked August 2nd, 1910.
(H.G. Allix, édit., Jersey)

Three views of Rozel...

To Mr & Mrs W. of Wanstead, London, 1954:

'Dear All,
Having a grand time. Weather is excellent. The Hotel is very good with plenty to eat. Drinks & cigs are cheap, so we are making the most of it. Flying to Guernsey next week for a day.

Ray & Molly'

Sent to Miss Vera Williams of Bangor, North Wales; postmarked 17 July, 1922:

'The White House, Rozel Bay

Hello, old top! How are you? I thought you might like a glimpse of Rozel so I am sending you this with an abundance of love. Cheerio! I shall be home on the <u>24th</u> so look out for a good time coming! We are having a gorgeous time here this next week, and last week we were booked up every day. I will tell you all about it when I come. Tomorrow we are anticipating a sail round the island. I am longing to see Mother and Daddie and you all again, but quite tearful at the thought of leaving this darling little isle and all my friends here.

My <u>very</u> best love to you and all.
Yours ever, Margo'

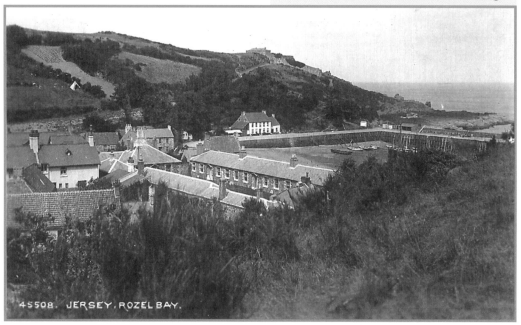

45508. JERSEY. ROZEL BAY.

128. Rozel Bay. An early 20th century view with Rozel barracks, built about 1810, in the foreground. The message on this card is given above right.
(Photochrom)

Rozel Bay, Jersey.

129. Rozel Bay. Postmarked 18 May 1931.

1163 ROZEL & TROPICAL GARDEN'S JERSEY.

BAY HOTEL.

130. Rozel & Tropical Gardens.

131. Bouley Bay. Postcard undated but, judging by the overprinted message, it dates from soon after the Liberation.
(The Halkett Series)

132. Bouley Bay. The Bouley Bay Hotel from the pier.
(Photochrom Co. Ltd., Tunbridge Wells)

133. Bonne Nuit Bay (J. Salmon, Sevenoaks)

134. Road from St. John's to Bonne Nuit Bay. Postmarked 19 June, 1939, addressed to Mrs Marsh of Kilburn, London: 'We are having a lovely time, wish you were here with us. The weather has been OK so far. Love from Chick.'
(Valentine & Sons, Ltd., Dundee and London)

Wolf Caves, Jersey.

135. Wolf's Caves

From Ward Lock Guide to the Channel Islands, 1921:

'There is a long and, to ladies, rather formidable descent by steep zig-zag paths almost to the foot of the deep ravine. Visitors are here met by a guide, who conducts them to an iron ladder leading down to the floor of the cave and obligingly lights a torch, so that the dimensions and the weirdness of the cave may be appreciated.'

The Devils Hole, Jersey. 479.

136. Stairway to the Devil's Hole. An Edwardian family making the dodgy looking descent. Such a manoeuvre would surely now be precluded by Health and Safety Regs.

(J. Welch & Sons, Portsmouth)

His Satanic Majesty, Devil's Hole, Jersey.
Le Grand, Nean Nea Xaculus.

137. Devil's Hole

From Ward Lock Guide to the Channel Islands, 1921:

'Rounding a dome-shaped hill, we reach a small refreshment bar. Here twopence is paid for the right of descent (much easier than in the case of the Wolf's Cave), and visitors can also see a caged black figure, with horns and tail, flap his wings and nod his head when a rope is pulled from the inside. Many visiting cards are left for his Satanic Majesty.'

In the Devils Hole, Jersey 1891.
Dans le trou de diable, Jersey.

138. 'In the Devil's Hole'

A barefoot maiden posed sitting on a rock and a couple standing on a rock surrounded by sea. The perspective here does not seem quite right – has the composition been faked?

(J. Welch & Sons, Portsmouth)

139. Memorial Stone, Marine Drive. Postmarked 2nd September, 1954. The North Coast Road was built by local unemployed men to provide work during the Occupation so it is a fitting site for this memorial stone, dedicated to the men and women of the Island who suffered during those years.
(Valentine & Sons, Ltd., Dundee and London)

✳

Message on card sent to Miss Neale of Holloway, London, in 1936:

'We have just paddled and watched the others bathe. Alas we are too sore to bathe ourselves, the sun has treated us very badly. Isn't Grève de Lecq pretty – we're thoroughly enjoying ourselves here'

✳

And so to Grève de Lecq...

140. Grève de Lecq. View from Le Chemin du Catel – the barracks in the foreground, the Pavilion Hotel (replaced in the 1970s by Caesar's Palace and, more recently, by a range of 'traditional' cottages), the Martello Tower and, to the right, the pier. Note also the little octagonal building with conical roof – just to the right of centre. This was a camera obscura, once a great attraction for tourists. It bore the legend, 'Come in and see England'. Only when the punters had entered did the guide introduce himself as 'Mr England'!
(Published by E.A. Schwerdtfeger & Co., London E.C. printed at their works in Berlin)

✳

MEMORIAL STONE, MARINE DRIVE, JERSEY. H.5178.

139.

140.

141. 'Grève de Lecq Caves'
Intrepid Edwardians exploring the rocks on the east side of the bay. (G.B.)

More of Grève de Lecq...

142. Featuring the Prince of Wales Hotel – compare its more developed state here with how it looks in no. 140. The hotel proprietor has hand-written on the back as follows:

'Terms with board
August 55/-   July 49/-
Other months 45/-
weekly each person.
Late dinner. Sep tables.
Electric light throughout.
Modern sanitation.
Comfortable Lounge.
Dining room overlooks the bay - a sea view with all meals.
Accommodation for 20 guests only.'

("Scotts" Photographers, Jersey)

✳

143. 'Old Barracks and Pavilion Hotel'. Undated but likely to be some time between the wars. The Pavilion Hotel was a handsome and characterful building until it burnt down in the mid-1970s. (The Dainty Series)

✳

144. Looking back towards the bay. Postmarked 2nd July, 1932. Addressed to Miss Collins of Teignmouth, Devon:

'Dear Mary,
Shall be arriving home late on Sat. night so will see you on Sun. unless taken ill in the meantime – doing my best to cope with too many late nights but no hopes.

Hilda'

✳

142.

143.

GREVE DE LECQ. JERSEY.

144.

Adventures at Plémont...

The Edwardians, like the Victorians, had a taste for the wilder side of nature, and this spirit is captured in the following six views:

145. Making the descent to Plemont, via the bridges, access for which a charge was levied. The remains of the concrete steps can be seen today. A hundred years ago the descent led directly to the most spectacular caves, rather than to the beach. This card bears the message:

'This afternoon we have been for a drive at Plemont & have had our tea at the little picnic house which you can see. We have already lost ourselves a few times. Will have a few things to tell you when I come back.
Au revoir, Frank'

146. Local porters were employed to carry the visitors and prevent them getting wet. The two local men – with flat caps and trim moustaches, look a good deal less chunky than their charges. And neither do they wear any form of clothing to protect them from the wet. Note how the lady is carried – the bearer has his arms firmly upright to support her beneath her shoulders. It is said that, if the receding tide did not leave many deep puddles, then the porters would dig them out to ensure their services were required by the next lot of visitors. (No attribution)

147. A busy scene on the beach and on the rocks at Plemont, but not a bathing costume, let alone boogie board, in sight.
(L.L. Printed in France)

145.

146.

From Ward Lock Guide to the Channel Islands, 1921:

'The most westerly cave is a little difficult of access even at low tide by reason of a pool. Hence the attendance of a number of stalwart bare-footed natives who for a coin of the realm are prepared to carry across any ladies who desire to go. There is really nothing remarkable to see when the trip has been made, but judging by the picture postcards passengers are fairly numerous.'

147.

Still at Plémont...

Message from a card sent 13/7/27, to Mr Counsell of Cardfiff:

'2, Edward Place, Royal Parade,
St. Helier, Jersey, C.I.

Dear Ed,
Having a real good time here. We visited Devil's Hole yesterday and also met him. It's very cold down there, but jolly hot climbing back. Took a snap of it, so hope it is a success. I can tell you we are getting quite experts at climbing. Had to climb 500 ft to see Wolfs Caves before we visited Devil's Hole. Then we went on to Grève de Lecq where there is a beautiful stretch of sands but we were swarmed with some kiddies from a creche who wanted to turn my bag inside out, but we moved on – nothing doing. The drive through country was glorious.   Agnes'

Message on card postmarked 30 September, 1953:

'This is a small island but it is full of good spots. Today we spent exploring the North Coast, with grand rocky cliffs and headlands and jolly little sandy coves. And what sand – acres & acres of it in some places – more than Richard could possibly fill with railways. Weather fine some days but always warm. A good time is being had by all. You would like the warm airs.

Love J'

148. 'Plémont Point – La Tête de Louis XIV' – in the distance.
Three decorous ladies paddling. The closest the Edwardian visitors in Jersey seemed to get to going in the sea.
(Photo G. Bridle – Jersey. Printed in France)

149. 'Une Traversée Amusante – A Pleasant Passage'.
The porters at work again: Note the lady, centre right, supported beneath her shoulders by a pair of upstretched arms, as in No.146; it must have been tough on the carriers!
(No attribution but 'Printed in France')

150. 'Plémont – The Waterfall – La Cascade'
Still flowing today and, mercifully, not diverted into a local reservoir.
(L.L. Printed in France)

An anonymous message, sent in 1922 to Mrs Barker of Dartford, Kent:

'Dear Mother,
We are stranded in a lighthouse owing to the rain. It turned out lovely yesterday. We have fine lodgings, the lady of the house is young & ever such a sport. I shouldn't be surprised if it doesn't stop raining all the holiday.'

152. L'Etacq.
View from another angle featuring "L'Etacquerel" Guest House, indicated by bold white arrow. The old Marina Bars can be see above the beach, now replaced with a development of holiday cottages.
Postmarked 30th August, 1957, addressed to Mr & Mrs Gibson of Stone, Staffordshire:

'Enjoying our holiday very much so hot in lovely sun. Have found a spot very like Wales for isolation but lovely beach. We have taken to cycling and are getting round very well now the wind has dropped.

Yrs. Betty'

151. L'Etacq, at Jersey's north-west corner.
(Photogravure Series. Foot, Jersey)

152.

153. St. Ouen's Bay from L'Etacq. The full sweep of the island's widest bay, from L'Etacq to Corbiere. Note the building extreme left middle distance: this is the Milano Bar, now demolished.
(Valentine & Sons Ltd., Dundee and London)

The south end of St. Ouen's Bay...

'Portelet Bay Holiday Camp
Jersey, C.I.

Dear Mrs & Mr Ramsden,
Just a few lines to let you know that
Betty and I are experiencing very
good weather and having an extremely
enjoyable time. The food here is
good, plentiful, and well cooked;
accommodation clean and comfortable, and scenery delightful.
Fruit is scarce, but we manage with
strawberries, raspberries, cherries
and ice cream, and of course unlimited
tomatoes. We shall be sorry when the
time to depart is due. Cheerio for now
and kindest regards.

Bill & Betty'

154. La Pulente.
Postmarked 2nd July, 1946, addressed
to Mrs & Mr Ramsden of Manchester. The
summer of 1946 was the first tourist season following the Liberation. The
correspondent is mindful of rationing at
home, as his message implies (left).
Photochrom Co. Ltd., London and Tunbridge
Wells)

*From Jersey Commercial Association
Guide, 1927:*
'The beach is an excellent one, and a
good road (known as the Five Mile Road),
runs almost the entire circuit of the bay;
here during the season may be seen the
vraic (seaweed) gatherers, men, women
and children gathering the harvest of the
sea, which is heaped into stacks after
being dried in the sun, and sold to
farmers as a fertiliser.'

154. The Five Mile Road, St. Ouen's Bay. Probably 1920s.

155. La Pulente. The southernmost reach of St. Ouen's Bay. The arched well can be seen beside the road on the right.
(No attribution but 'British Manufacture')

156. La Pulente.

And so to Corbiere, one of Jersey's most famous landmarks...

LE PHARE DE LA CORBIÈRE.

5222. JERSEY. CORBIÈRE LIGHTHOUSE.

157. Corbière Lighthouse with fisherman. He has a net and a bag hanging from his waist to store any shrimps he may catch. He is wearing gumboots so is well equipped.
(Exclusive Celesque Series. Photo-chrom Co. Ltd., London and Tun-bridge Wells)

158. View with Edwardian visitors.
Corbière Lighthouse was built in 1873. It was the first light-house to be built of concrete; the tower is 35 feet high.
(Published by Labey & Son,
  The Beresford Library, Jersey)

158.

159. No postmark but, judging by the message, sent soon after Liberation; addressed to Miss Roche in Wolverhampton:

'We had a very rough crossing. Both very ill. Visiting relatives most of the time so far. They have had a dreadful time. They can't really believe that it is all over.'

(J. Salmon Ltd., Sevenoaks)

⁕

160. An atmospheric moonlit view.
(Glossy Photo Series. The Photo-chrome Co. Ltd.,
London)

Jersey. Corbiere Lighthouse. Moonlight.   C.N.

160.

Still at Corbière...

From Jersey Commerical Association Guide, 1927:

'No visit to Jersey is complete unless La Corbière is visited; there are frequent trains; those desiring to walk part of the way should alight at La Haule Station, and walk up La Haule Hill, one of the prettiest roads in Jersey, with its cuttings through the rock and overhanging trees. Cyclists and those driving or motoring should also take this road.'

Message on card sent in 1952 to Mr & Mrs Butler of Itchen, Southampton:

'Dear Mum & Pop,
Well we arrived here dead tired 5.30 this morning. The place is very nice, food good so far and what a lovely bedroom. Cliff is in heaven just shorts on sun-bathing after a swim.
Love Beryl XXX'

I have a poor quality postcard of Corbière, not reproduced here. Like no. 159, it was posted soon after Liberation. It was written by a local, not a visitor, so is not strictly within the scope of this book, but is nevertheless worth quoting. Addressed to Mr & Mrs G. of Havant, Hampshire, the message makes poignant reading:

'Looking at snaps taken in '38 reminds me you might be at this address. Am here on Aug. 7th. Leave after 7 years at home 6 Cheapside, St. Helier. All at Cheapside well considering Jean & Clem quite grown up, new addition to family, Carol age 4 yrs cute blond thing. Weather still as perfect as ever but poor island looking very delapidated after 5 years occupation, most Bays ruined. Arthur & Frankie send best regards. Hope you are both well, much love
Betty'

JERSEY—CÔTE PRÈS DE LA CORBIÈRE — COAST SCENE NEAR CORBIÈRE

161. Thatched tea rooms at Corbière ("F.F." Jersey)

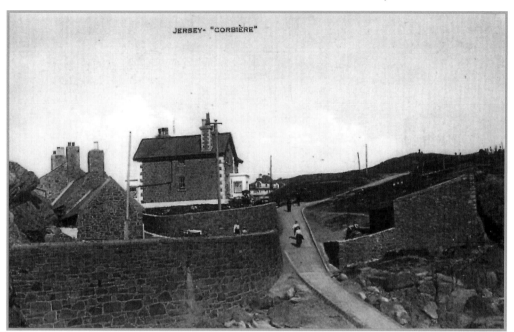

162. Corbière.
("F.F." Jersey)

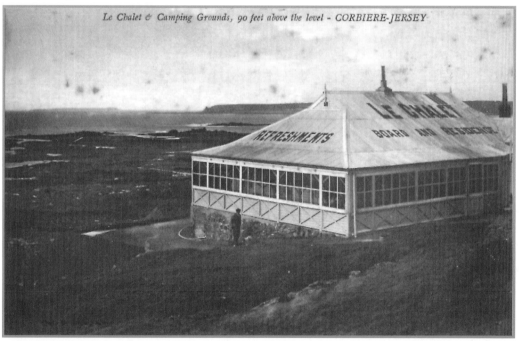

163. 'Le Chalet & Camping Grounds, 90 feet above sea level. This must represent an earlier view than that depicted in no.33, the latter showing developemnt of the Le Chalet Hotel.
(No attribution but 'Printed in France')

St. Brelade's Bay, many would say Jersey's finest; a place which has certainly inspired postcard correspondents. For example...

'My Dear Dad,
Although I have only just begun my holiday, I am having quite a good time. So far the weather in behaving well, but not quite up to scratch yet. You'd love Jersey, it's very beautiful, and the sea so blue, but you want to be a good walker to reap the full benefit. Already I have walked a long way, but there's so much to see, you forget about being tired. I went to this little Bay on Saturday afternoon, can you imagine stretches of golden sand, surrounded with deep blue water, & rugged rocks, & in the background hills covered with yellow gorse, it's a picture. I've met some very nice people at the Hotel, but we are only 12 in all. Will send more cards soon, Heaps of love to Mum, & yourself dears, Evie.'

Postmarked 11th May, 1931 and addressed to O. Smith Esq. of South Godstone, Surrey.

※

Message to Mr Brown of Winchester:

'We apparently do not know what sunshine, surf & also rain are in England. Here everything is on an enlarged scale. We are having a truly great time. Had to shelter on the hill here from a waterspout. Some fine Janes here.'

164. Postmarked September 24th, 1909.
(J. Welch & Sons, Photographic Publishers, Portsmouth)

165. No postmark but probably post-World War 2
(R.A. (Postcards) Ltd., London, E.C.4)

✳

And here are two more, the first addressed to Mrs Battrick of Manchester:

'Biarritz Hotel
24.9.64

Despite warning of strong head winds resulting in longer flight time arrived at airport at 12.30. It's absolutely tropical here – backless cotton frocks in the drawing room & sun worshippers lying along the balcony looking like walnuts (in colour!). I don't know if I told you that this hotel is a Methodist Holiday Home & seems full. I think you would like it here. Sorry about the bad writing – new biro seems to make me wobble! Regards to all.'

✳

'Dear Friends,
Just to let you know we arrived safely. Having a wonderful holiday. Did a coach trip today all around the Island. All the different bays and beaches are wonderful, the Glass Church, and all the fortifications from the German Occupation. Cheerio. See you Sunday.'

Postmarked 12th September, 1962

166. St. Brelade's Bay, looking a good deal less cluttered than it does today.
(J. Salmon Ltd., Sevenoaks)

167. St. Brelade's Bay. Postmarked 16th September, 1953. Note the sea wall, a relic of the German Occupation.

168. Ouaisné Bay. Postmarked 194?
(R.A. (Postcards) Ltd., London, E.C.4)

169. Ouaisné Bay. Shack-like dwellings, now largely vanished, nicely reflected in the wet sand. Postmarked 7th September, 1934 and addressed to Monsieur & Madame Max Picard in Rouen, France.

170. Portelet Bay.
Postmarked 11th June, 1951, addressed to Miss M Sanders of Bristol:

'We arrived quite safely. The boat trip was lovely and the others enjoyed the 'plane journey. the weather is good & the hotel all that could be desired. We like it on the island very much.
Yours sincerely, F. Phillips'

(Salmon, Sevenoaks)

From Ward Lock's Guide, 1937:

'The increasing popularity of Portelet is evidenced by the rapidly increasing number of bungalows and holiday camps, where, away from all charabanc routes, visitors can dress as they please and lead the simple life.'

171. Noirmont Point.
Postmarked 1909, addressed to Miss Jenny Young of Innerleithen, Scotland:

'We came on here today from St. Malo. The island is lovely. Ideal place for a honeymoon. I said so! So note this down! Weather is mid-summer broiling hot. Nevertheless we are fairly active and mean to see (comfortably) what is to be seen.'

(Photochrom Co. Ltd., London and Detroit, USA)

Message on postcard sent in 1934 to Miss N Simm of Bournemouth:

'We passed this today [Portelet] and are at present sat in the rocks almost like an armchair only of course without the cushions. We have done a good deal of climbing and scrambling.
Love from May'

JANVRIN'S TOMB, PORTELET BAY, JERSEY.   18937.

170. Portelet Bay.

171. Noirmont Point.

172. Belcroute Bay. One of Jersey's less frequented coastal spots, though it looks fairly idyllic in this view.

St. Aubin, never as large a town as St. Helier, but an important port before the completion of St. Helier's new quay in the nineteenth century...

173. St. Aubin. An unusual view from Noirmont Woods. Postmarked 27th August 1935, addressed to Miss C Stewart of Edinburgh:

'Having a good holiday. Weather perfect. Plenty of fun. Was a bit sick on the boat coming but it was worth it all.

Vera'

174. St Aubin from West. Postmarked 8th August, 1914, addressed to Mr E Hancock of Dorchester, Dorset:

'Dear Cousin
I am very sorry I was unable to call on Friday evening, as I was on the rush until Sat. to catch the boat. It is nothing but war here.'

This card was posted four days after the declaration of World War I.
Note the railway track approaching St. Aubin's Station (formerly the Terminus Hotel and now St. Brelade's Parish Hall) and the Corbière line to the right making a sharp right hand bend.
(Valentine's Series)

St. Aubins, Jersey.

173.

St. Aubins from West

174.

ST. AUBIN'S, JERSEY.   2080

175. St. Aubin's. View across the harbour towards St. Brelade's Parish Hall. Postmarked 9th June, 1952.
(R.A. (Postcards) Ltd., London, E.C.4)

176 (right). St. Aubin's High Street. A peaceful prospect down the unimproved High Street. Sent to a Miss Cadogan (no date or postmark):

'This gives a pretty good idea of the "One Way" traffic at St. Aubin's, hope the crowds don't make you feel giddy. Don't be too lazy, my child, I like to picture you working hard!
B. Lowcliffe'

(Judges Ltd., Hastings)

177. Looking towards town before the age of the infernal combustion engine! Note the sign outside the former railway station on the right which says STATION ENTRANCE. (It does – I've checked the original with a magnifying glass.) Also the grocery shop on the left BERESFORD SUPPLY STORES. This became ORVISS, then LE RICHE, and is now renamed, somewhat inelegantly, STAMPERS.
(F.F., Jersey)

6902 St AUBINS HIGH St. JERSEY · JUDGES' L^{TD}

178. St. Aubin's.
card sent to Mr & Mrs B of Seaford, postmarked 8 August, 1956:

'Dear Mr & Mrs B
We are all having a wonderful time. The weather has been glorious. Its been about 80° today. Hope you have a nice time
Yours sincerely, DHR'

(Raphael Tuck)

Message on card postmarked 20 June 1927, to Mr P Gomes of Kingston on Thames, Surrey:

'My Dear Phil,
How are things going? Alright I hope: Saturday night was the time of our lives. I was glad to see daylight. Everything is quite nice now. Marie & Fred have gone a trip today. The cars come to the door & gather the people, fine isn't it! So is the weather.
Love Mum'

177.

178.

179. Approaching La Haule – see the beach hut proclaiming TEAS, now sadly closed. The beach had visitors in those days; today it is a no-go zone thanks to the plague of sea lettuce which invades each summer. Posted 22nd August 1959 and sent to Miss C of Bath:

'Weather still grand. Thunderstorm from 10.30 om through the night. No other rain at all. Overcast this morning. Just going to the park. A ride yesterday afternoon. Good TV reception here. Think Mrs S cat run over this morning. 3 more in today. 7 altogether now...

Love Doll'

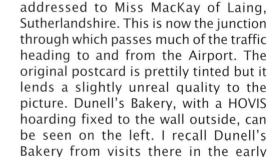

181. Beaumont. Postmarked in 1909, addressed to Miss MacKay of Laing, Sutherlandshire. This is now the junction through which passes much of the traffic heading to and from the Airport. The original postcard is prettily tinted but it lends a slightly unreal quality to the picture. Dunell's Bakery, with a HOVIS hoarding fixed to the wall outside, can be seen on the left. I recall Dunell's Bakery from visits there in the early 1950s.

180. La Haule Lane.
Leading directly to the slipway seen in no. 179.
(F.F., Jersey)

181. Beaumont.

182. First Tower. The Martello Tower is supporting a water tank which in turn is surmounted by a windmill, used to pump water to fill the tank. The whole elaborate structure must have posed a hazard in high winds. Pedestrians strolling in the traffic-free road. Undated but presumably pre-First World War.
(J. Welch & Sons, Photographic Publishers, Portsmouth)

Message on card sent in 1956 and addressed to 'Reception, Messrs. Knox & Hardy Ltd., London, EC4':

'Dear Inmates,

Having a grand time (Don't wish you were here!!!) The hotel is a great place. We have got quite tanned especially the last few days. Hope everything's under control at your end and you are not working too hard. Don't let Mr B illtreat you.

Kind regards to all.
Cheerio, Audrey'

Attractions

Jersey's major attractions, so far as the holidaymaker is concerned, include its climate (generally more favourable than the mainland), its beaches, coastline and countryside, together with its proximity to France and its consequent 'differentness' to British resorts. As if all this were not enough, a number of tourist attractions, of varied quality, developed throughout the rise of mass tourism in the last century.

Guide books consistently recommended tours of the island which took in the best of the coastal and inland scenery. A high point of these tours was a stop at Prince's Tower, which stood above La Hougue Bie and which afforded 'a good view from the top over about two-thirds of the Island.' The Prince's Tower was demolished shortly after the excavation of La Hougue Bie and the discovery that it is a prehistoric site of major importance.

One of the foremost attractions of pre-war days were the so-called Troglodyte Caves at Five Oaks. A guide book in 1921 comments, a touch unconvincedly: 'Troglodyte Caves is an instance of what can be done with shells, stones, a little lake and a few mud walls. Some visitors find a quaint interest here, others are amused, and others again are not.'

During the heyday of the 1950s there were three main attractions to which the motor coaches carried visitors: the Glass Church at Millbrook, the German Underground Hospital in St Peter's and the German Occupation Museum at La Hougue Bie. And that was about it until the opening of many others in later years, like Jersey Zoo and the Lavender Farm. Jersey Museums have latterly done a wonderful job of presenting the varied strands of the island's history in an informative, entertaining and highly professional manner at various historic sites around the island..

183. Druids Alter.

Not a 'Druids Alter' at all, or even a 'Druids' Altar', this is a Dolmen, or burial chamber, which would once have been covered in earth so as appear as a great mound.

Postmarked August 24th 1904, addressed to Miss Drew of Holborn, London:

> 'Dear Glad,
> Am having a very nice time. Weather lovely – plenty of "Francais" but do not want any of them. Nearly all fellows in the house.
>
> Love May'

(JWS 1059)

※

184. Prince's Tower, St. Martin's, erected towards the end of the eighteenth century . Used as an observation post during the French Wars, formerly surmounted the chapel on the summit of the mound known as La Hougue Bie. Demolished in 1924, the Prince's Tower, with the magnificent views over much of the island to which it gave access, was once a magnet for every visitor to Jersey. Since 1919 the mound – claimed to be the finest dolmen in Western Europe – has been explored by the Société Jersiaise, though its archaeological significance was not realised until 1924. It is now open to the public under the auspices of the Jersey Museums Service, together with other attractions at the same site.

(Geo. Barré, Jersey)

※

Druids Alter, Jersey. Sav! Jackie looks rather lonely!

183.

184.

185. The Well, La Hougue Bie
(Société Jersiaise)

The Well, La Hougue Bie.

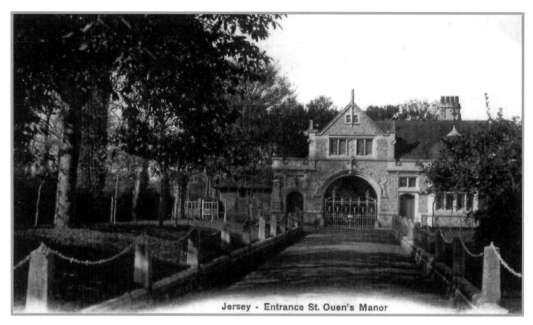

Jersey - Entrance St. Ouen's Manor

186. St. Ouen's Manor.
Not sent home by a visitor but sent by a local to a friend to boost her postcard collection. Posted in 1904 to Miss Le Boutillier of St Helier:

'Dear Gladys
I am sending you this Pc to put in your collection.

                    With love, A Le B'

✳

Message on card postmarked 4 September, 1933 to Mrs Dewar of Ruislip, Middlesex:

'Dear Mo

Arrived at 7.15, had a lovely trip across, the weather has been glorious. Roy has struck lucky, there is a boy his own age, no other children here. We went to a dance at the new Pavilion last night 8.30 until 12 o'clock. Sports tomorrow. Weather is still very hot. Love to all.

                    Clive'

From Ward Lock's Guide, 1937, this description of West Park Pavilion:

'This magnificent "Palais de Danse", the building equal to and the setting more delightful than anything London can show, was opened in July, 1931. The terrace in front is a delightful spot for refreshments during the Thés Dansants. The interior is equally pleasing, being tastefully decorated and furnished, and prettily lighted. The floor is excellent, and will comfortably accommodate 200 to 250 couples.'

✳

187. The Opera House, in Gloucester Street, opened in 1900 by Jerseywoman and internationally famous actress, Lillie Langtry. Completely restored and reopened in 2000.

188. West Park Pavilion. Opened in 1931, the 'Pav' replaced an earlier building known as 'The Tin Hut'. Demolished in 2001 to be replaced by luxury apartments. Postmarked 6th July, 1951, and sent to Finisterre, France.
(Valentine & Sons., Dundee and London)

The Battle of Flowers, an annual summer event which began in 1902...

Message on card postmarked August 8, 1907, to Master W Bond of Wellington, Somerset:

'We are going to 'Battle of Flowers' a grand fête in front of West Park this afternoon when prizes are given for best decorated cars, vans etc. Tons of flowers will be used on some of these devices & at conclusion they tear them off & throw at spectators on stands & vice versa – We go to Guernsey Sat morn leaving 9am.'

From Jersey booklet published by Chamber of Commerce, 1955.

'Spectacular Setting, Breath-taking Exhibits, Lavishly Decorated Arena, A real Spirit of Carnival'

BATTLE OF FLOWERS, JERSEY, JULY 26th, 1906.   *Albert Smith, Photo., Jersey.*

189. The 1906 Battle of Flowers. Garlands and Chinese lanterns decorate Victoria Avenue.
(Albert Smith, Photo. Jersey)

190. The 1909 Battle of Flowers.
(Albert Smith, Photographer, Broad and New Street, Jersey)

191. Solemn-faced girls dressed up to take part in the 1912 Parade.

Message on a card postmarked 29 August, 1950, sent to Miss J. Bracegirdle of Newbury, Berkshire:

'Having grand time. Daddy & I went to service at the Church of Glass last Sunday. It was beautiful cannot express its beauty. We have just had a tour of the Island. We are just going in a party of 28 to the Esplanade. Table reserved by the Hotel.

Cheerio Love Mother XXX

Message to Mr Taylor of Sunderland, 1935:

'Dear Lummy,
The telephones here seem to be hopeless at night. I tried to get through Sunday but it was no use.'

Message to Mrs W Andrews of Croydon (undated):

'The weather is really grand here in fact we look like a couple of roast chickens already.'

Love Ruth

192. Troglodyte Caves, Five Oaks, St. Saviour's. (H J R Le Brun, Rozel, Jersey)

From a guide book published in 1899:

'Troglodyte Caves, Five Oaks, are well worth a visit. Here are to be seen a series of small caves skilfully lined with shells, as well as ornamental waters and nicely-kept grounds; the whole reflecting great credit upon the perseverance and patience of the proprietor. Music and refreshments are both provided.'

193. Fort Regent Entrance. The keystone above the arch records the date 1806 and the initials of King George III. This massively built defensive structure was erected during the Napoleonic Wars and used as a parade ground by the Jersey Militia for many years. The whole complex was abandoned following Liberation but was eventually redeveloped in the 1960s as the Fort Regent Leisure Centre. (The "Beresford" Series)

✳

194. (below). 'St. Sauveur – Corps de Garde du Gouverneur' Guards, whose uniforms resemble those of policemen, outside the Governor's residence in St. Saviour. ('Printed in France')

Jersey - Entrance Fort Regent

JERSEY. - St-Sauveur. - Corps de garde du Gouverneur

Life expectancy was a great deal less a century ago, and the many orphans were cared for in orphanages, important institutions and sometimes impressive buildings, worthy of postcard status and a mention in contemporary guide books...

195. Female Orphans' Home, Grouville.

196. Dr. Barnardo's Homes for Little Boys, Gorey.

ST. MATTHEWS CHURCH, MILLBROOK.

197. St. Matthew's Church,
Millbrook, St. Lawrence.
The church was reconstructed and
rededicated in 1934 in memory of
Lord Trent, founder of Boots the
Chemists. Containing many features
in Lalique glass, St. Matthew's be-
came known as 'The Glass Church'

198. Altar, St. Matthew's Church.
Postmarked 15th August, 1948, and
sent to Miss Bushy of Sloane Street,
London:

'Dear Miss Bushy,
We are having a fine time, the
weather is lovely but this last
week the wind has been very
strong & cold so have not spent a
lot of time on the beach.
This is the Altar of the Glass
Church, it is very nice inside.'

187.

ALTAR, ST. MATTHEWS CHURCH MILLBROOK, JERSEY.

199.

199. German Underground Hospital. Countless thousands of holidaymakers have visited here since it opened to the public soon after Liberation. It was stripped of the majority of its fixtures and fittings after Liberation, no doubt in a fit of wanting to get rid of everything to do with those five dark years, with the exception of heavy items like the air conditioning plant featured in no. 201. It was a largely empty and rather spooky place for many years – see below, and not particularly edifying for the visitor.

Message on card sent in 1947 to Rev & Mrs A Simmons of Halifax:

'Dear Auntie Hilda & Uncle Albert, Just a hurried card to tell you how grand I have found your old home. I expect you would find a lot of changes, however, the people are still A1 in spite of their troubles.
Michael'

Transverse Corridor—German Underground Hospital.
—St. Peter, Jersey.

200.

201. German Underground Hospital
(Photo Precision Ltd., St. Albans.)

202.Corbière Lighthouse and German Look-Out Post. In this view the lighthouse is dwarfed by the later structure which the occupiers attempted to disguise as a granite building, though its style is hardly in the Jersey vernacular tradition. (M & L)

Jersey's attractive old-world inns, many of them former farmhouses, are dotted around the island and were a favourite destination for evening tours, sometimes designated 'Mystery Tours'...

A message from 1947:

'Jersey is wonderful. We'll live here when we are old.'

A message from 1958:

'Dear Dortothy
Having a lovely time here. Been all over the island. Spent every afternoon on hot sands at St Brelades Bay. Both brown. In evenings seen 18 show bars and french shows. All so clean & smart & different to home. Good cosy hotel. Friendly people.

Love from Fred & Marion'

Message on card postmarked 24 August, 1953, sent to Miss R of Christchurch, Hampshire:

'Had a fairly rough crossing and the sun seems to have deserted us. So have mostly gone shopping. We are having wonderful food so shall be really fat when we come home.

Bud'

THE BLUE BAR - ST. PETER'S WINDMILL - JERSEY, C.I.

191. The Blue Bar, St. Peter's Windmill. This 'old inn' is located in a former windmill.

204. L'Auberge du Nord, St. John.
A charming and genuinely old building in a spacious and windswept location near the north coast.
(Eversheds, St. Albans)

205. Cockatoo called Laura in the Fisherman's Bar, Dolphin Hotel, Gorey Pier, St. Martin. No doubt a source of amusement and caused nipped fingers to customers.

Rough Sea, Jersey.

206. Rough Sea, seen here at La Collette. Always an attraction (except when visitors were travelling by boat), a spectacle remarked upon in many postcards sent home.

Message on a postcard sent home in 1920:

This is a sample of what I am experiencing. It is really dreadful. I went to Sark yesterday. So bad the sailors had to hold on to the railing for fear of being washed overboard.

Country Jersey

The British have long held a nostalgic attachment to what they imagine is the traditional way of life of the countryside. This predilection could be freely indulged in Jersey, with its miniature fields and narrow lanes overhung with trees, its small-scale mixed farming; indeed, its fundamentally peasant economy.

Tours to explore inland Jersey, first by horse-drawn carriage, later by motor charabanc and then by motor coach, have long been an enticement to visitors desirous of experiencing the charms of the Jersey countryside.

The island's valleys give access from low-lying St. Helier to the green and hilly hinterland. A guide book published in 1921 notes that: 'Jersey has about a dozen valleys of surpassing loveliness and charm, valleys through which it is a constant delight to walk or drive.'

Perhaps the most frequented valley was that of St. Peter's, as the many postcards which feature it testify. A drive up this valley would perhaps take tourists to Vinchelez Lane in St. Ouen's, which was particularly celebrated for its rural charm. The unromantically named Waterworks Valley was already, at the beginning of the last century, under development as a site for reservoirs, but the advent of man-made bodies of water seemed to form an added attraction. Vallée des Vaux was also much visited and even Bellozane Valley in the days before rubbish disposal became its preoccupation.

Thatched and pantiled farm buildings, tethered Jersey cows grazing contentedly at the roadside, milkmaids in the fields squatting on three-legged milking stools with traditional spherical milk cans, alarmingly sloping côtils alive with Jersey Royals, fields full of tomatoes tied to wooden crosses looking like verdant graveyards, amazing Jersey cabbages like something out of fairy tale, heaps of pongy seaweed waiting to be used as fertiliser – all these added to the fascination of visitors in country Jersey.

Message on card postmarked 5 August, 1914 (a day after the declaration of war) to Miss D Fraser of Sale, Cheshire:

'How are you getting on? Hope the pupils are quite satisfactory. Things are getting lively here! We may be poor but we <u>do</u> see life! What terrible things are happening! We shall probably come home much earlier than was intended. One service (Weymouth) is stopped.

L.G.'

Message on card postmarked 24 June, 1924:

'We have been for a lovely ride this morning and went through this lane [Vinchelez Lane]. We are now sitting on some rocks overlooking the sea. We are having a picnic lunch and this afternoon intend having a bathe from the sands – there aren't many people about.   Best Love, Ella'

209. St. John's Lane.
Postmarked August 24th, 1908, addressed to Miss Lees of Sloane Street, London:

'29 Havre-des-Pas

Is this not a pretty lane, we went through it on our way to Plémont it is one of the prettiest pieces I have seen on the island. How did you like [?] & did you have fine weather? Have you learnt to swim? We are just opposite the bathing pool & it is great fun to watch the swimming & diving some of it from a board 25ft above the water.

K.L.G.'

(Geo. Barré, Jersey)

229   JERSEY. — *Vinchelez Lane.* — LL.

207. Vinchelez Lane, St. Ouen. (L.L. Printed in France)

208. St. Mary's. (J. Welch & Sons, Portsmouth. Printed in Saxony)

67 — **Jersey** - Sᵗ John's Lane

209. St John's Lane.

Message on a card postmarked 28 September, 1937, to Miss Bruce of Leytonstone, London:

'Dear Auntie,

We have just come over here for a week, the weather is glorious. I was rather disappointed in the Island. I expected to see beautiful scenery. We had a very good crossing, the sea was calm all the way.
With love to Grannie & yourself.

Dolly'

Dolly the ingrate had enjoyed both a good crossing and fine weather but was still not satisfied (Ed.)

✳

A breathless message on a card sent to Mr & Mrs B. of Lewes:

'Dear Joan & Ron

We are enjoying our holiday good weather plenty of cheap booze and plenty of interesting places to visit we had a trip round the island its beautiful and we are enjoying the night life but time is going so quickly.

See you soon, Rose & Eric'

✳

From Ward Lock's Guide to the Channel Islands, 1920:

'Rozel Lane, an exquisite bit of scenery. The trees arch overhead, and below the white railings on either side of the road is a leafy glen, with a lake glistening through the leaves on the right-hand side. The coaches pause for a minute here.'

210. A Quiet Nook is St. Mary's. (F.F., Jersey)

211. Rozel Lane. St. Martin. (Albert Smith, photo. Jersey)

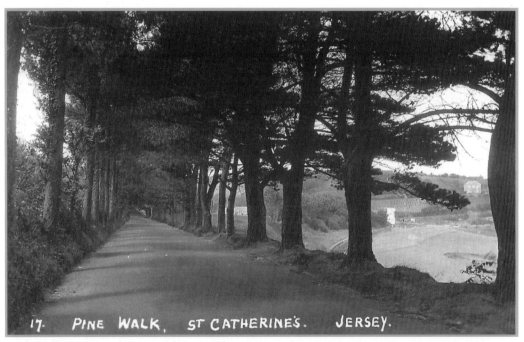

212. Pine Walk, St. Catherine's. This is the road more properly known as La Mont de la Mare. See through the trees on the right to the Martello Tower and slipway at La Mare.

Church and Chapel...

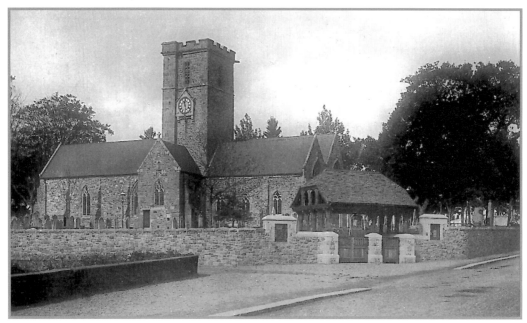

213. St. Saviour's Church. Lillie Langtry lies in its graveyard.
(Pitt Series No 29)

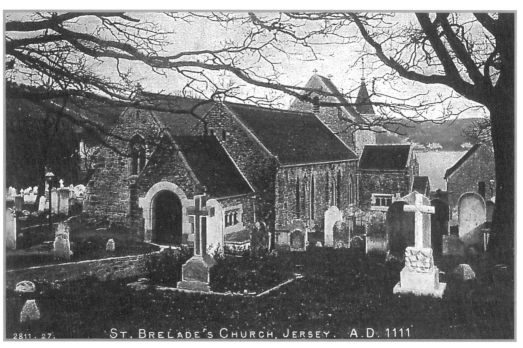

214.

Jersey has 12 parish churches; two of the country parish churches are pictured opposite. In addition to these and a scattering of Roman Catholic churches, Jersey has many nonconformist chapels, mainly Wesleyan Methodist.

214. St. Brelade's Church. A.D. 1111

The only one of the island's 12 Parish Churches located above the shore, though the Town Church in St Helier was once much closer to the sea before land was reclaimed and harbours constructed. St. Brelade's thus possesses the shortest sanctuary path, providing a means of escape from the sanctuary of the church to that of the open sea.

1196 WESLEYAN CHAPEL, ST. OUEN'S, JERSEY.

215. Wesleyan Chapel, St. Ouen's.

John Wesley visited the Channel Islands in 1787 and preached all over Jersey, mainly in French. He found many people willing to hear his message and join his congregation. From humble origins, some fine chapels were erected throughout the island. Many are still active, though others lie idle with the shrinkage of the chapel-going population.

St. Peter's Valley, perhaps Jersey's most celebrated...

216. Sent in 1906 to Miss Hoddinott of Sherborne, Dorset. Is that the photographer's bicycle propped up against the bank to the right?
(J. Welch & Sons, Portsmouth. Printed at our works in Belgium)

217. A view featuring the Victoria Hotel, rebuilt in the 1970s and now just a pub. (L.L. Printed in France)

218. (L.L. Printed in France)

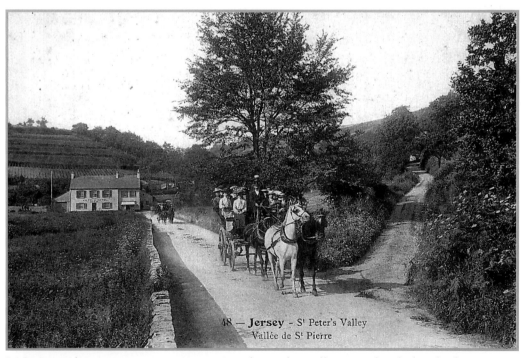

219. A two-horse excursion car coming down the Valley, another behind. The Victoria Hotel in the distance.

220. Entrance to Bellozanne Valley. The place-name Bellozanne is now synonymous with waste disposal and is one of several valleys leading down to St. Aubin's Bay. *Ward Lock's Guide* in 1937 notes that 'It is unfortunate that a destructor should have been placed here: it spoils a lovely view.'

146. - Jersey. - St-HÉLIER - Vallée des Vaux - E. D.

221.

222. Sent to Miss Danbury of Acton, London:

'Had a perfect voyage. Sea calm. Sunshine glorious. Am already feeling rested. Hope you will have a glorious holiday.

With love. Yours sincerely'

223. In Valley des Vaux. (J. Welch & Sons, Portsmouth. Printed in Germany)

Waterworks Valley, the first of the Island's valleys to be flooded as a mean of water supply. The old name, 'Les Chemins des Moulins' recalls an earlier time when the streams flowing down St. Lawrence Valley turned the wheels of several watermills...

225. 'In the Water Valley'.
Postmarked 28th September 1923, addressed to M Harrington of Rum Quay, West India Docks, London E:

'Dear Frank
Having a perfect time over here, weather glorious.
Kind regards to all.

Tubby'

(J. Welch & Sons, Portsmouth)

224. Postmarked 12th August, 1926, addressed to Miss Lily Kay in Ontario, Canada:

'Having a nice quiet holiday here. Lovely weather and good company.

Best love from Uncle Dick.'

225.

226. 'Gathering berries in The Water Valley'. One wonders whether the lady on the left is steadying her companion or about to push her in.
(J. Welch & Sons, Portsmouth)

At Anne Port.   W.   .

227.

227. 'At Anne Port'.
Postmarked July 14th, 1910, addressed to Mrs Servio of Shepherd's Bush, London:

'We are quite near Anne Port. Such a pretty place. Ada came yesterday and we went thro' on the way back with her. We have had a lovely walk this morning thro' the lanes. The country is all very pretty & green.
                    Love to both, D & H'

(No attribution)

✳

From 'Know Jersey', 1965:

'The island of Jersey is basically a farming community. Tourists flock on to the beaches but few go inland, which is a pity, for they miss some beautiful country scenes.'

✳

Message on card postmarked August 12, 1912, to Mr Wood of New Malden, Surrey:

'I was sick coming over it was so rough. I hope it won't be rough when you cross. We had a beautiful day yesterday but it is raining now. With love from all.
                    Beryl'

228. Old Farm House - Mont-au-Prêtre.
This is the old Poingdestre Farm. Note the thatched roofs, once commonly used as roofing material in the country. Sent in 1904 to Miss Kinnear of Fife, Scotland. (The "Beresford" Series)

229. 'Ivy Well, Trinity'.

230. A Jersey Mill in Winter.
(Albert Smith Ltd., Jersey)

Messages from a series of three post-cards written and posted on consecutive days to Mr & Mrs H. of Manchester. They were mailed in mid-July, 1952, but bear King George VI postage stamps, even though this was some weeks after Queen Elizabeth II had ascended to the throne:

'Friday 8am
My Dear Mum & Dad,
Thanks for letter received yesterday morning. Had a game of tennis with two people from the Hotel yesterday morning. Went to the Bay pictured on the other side [Bonne Nuit] in the afternoon. Weather was warm but cloudy. Had a wee dip and quite enjoyed it. It is only about half an hour's run to most of the bays from St. Helier. Sorry Rusty kept you awake at the weekend. Hope you are both well.'

'Saturday
Had a morning round town this morning. Lovely and sunny with a slight breeze. Went to the bay pictured overleaf [St. Brelade's] this afternoon. The beach is not very nice at St. Helier but it is a very good centre for getting around. I see it must have been raining in M/C yesterday as there wasn't any cricket. Take care of yourselves.'

'Sunday
Just arrived back from a coach tour to the German Underground Hospital, St. Peter's Valley, Plemont, L'Etacq and the Glass Church. Today has been strong sun but a very strong wind with it. Played tennis with Maisie & Ray again this morning. Very enjoyable. Then we walked back along the beach. The tide was in and the sea was quite choppy. Hope you are both well and have had no more storms.

Lots of love, Marjorie'

Message on card postmarked 16 September 1953, to Miss D Barnes of Eastbourne:

'Dear Doreen,
I went up to tennis last week, but as you didn't turn up I presumed that you thought I was on holiday. However, I actually only started last Saturday & so will not be home until the 26th September. My transfer is fixed for the end of October so I hope we will get a few games of squash in before then. The weather here has been putrid, we have only been on the beach for one morning. We went overleaf [St Brelade's Bay] yesterday and it is very beautiful – not much inland – very like Surrey but coast is wonderful.

Be seeing you, Ann.'

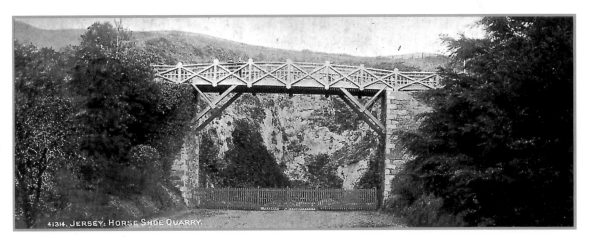

231. Horse Shoe Quarry (approx. 65% size of original).
Quarries are perhaps not the most obvious destination for tourists. However, Edwardian travellers were generally more adventurous than we are today. Whilst they admired Jersey's coastscapes and the charms of its valleys and rural scenery, they also had an eye for the advances of industry and social progress – hence the fascination of Waterworks Valley, where the water purification plant was as much admired as the wooded valley sides. And they visited quarries, like this one, from which granite was used for the Thames Embankment, a fact which no doubt impressed visitors.
('Panoramic Card' from Photochrom Co. Ltd., London & Detroit, U.S.A.)

232. Old Jersey Cider Press. More properly called an apple crusher, this was a vital tool in the once important cider industry. Massively built of granite (most commonly stone from Chausey, in several curved sections). Many examples are still to be seen around the island, often making a feature in someone's front garden. When in use, a horse would have been harnessed to drag the wheel around the trough. (A.G.L.M. Jersey)

Farming Jersey

Life in a small island encourages self-sufficiency. In Jersey the riches of the sea are complemented by those of the land. Jersey generally possesses well drained, easily worked soil traditionally enriched with seaweed, or *vraic*, which compensated for a lack of lime. The fame of Jersey's agricultural products is out of all proportion to the size of the island: Jersey Royal potatoes, the Jersey cow and its rich milk products, and Jersey tomatoes are all well known. Formerly the island was a major producer of apples and cider, both for consumption at home and export.

Today, like the situation in mainland Britain and, to a lesser extent, throughout Europe, Jersey's agriculture is in sharp decline. The island herd has diminished greatly in recent years. Not so long ago the typical Jersey smallholding possessed eight or a dozen cows and one would frequently see a beast or two tethered in a field or at the roadside to graze a small patch of grass. Today the island's cows are concentrated in a few large herds. Indeed, horses are now a more common sight in rural Jersey than cows – and they are definitely not working horses but horses, or ponies, used for leisure.

Where once it seemed that every square inch of the island was carefully husbanded, now fields lie fallow and neglected. The cultivation of outdoor tomatoes, planted immediately the potatoes were lifted, peaked between the wars, but fields full of tomato plants tied to wooden crosses were still a familar sight until relatively recently. Now, even the more intensive growing of greenhouse tomatoes is under threat.

Holidaymakers, in their trips around the island, were wont to admire the productiveness of the countryside and, of course, this is a feature which still draws admiration. But the picturesque smallholding, which supported an extended family with the aid of seasonal labour, is a thing of the past.

Note traditional spherical milk cans in nos 234 and 235, also the traditional sun bonnets that all four ladies are wearing...

233. Butter-making (LL)

TYPICAL JERSEY.

211 CHANNEL ISLANDS. — *Butter-making.*
Iles Anglo-Normandes. — *Le Barratage du Beurre.* — LL.

234. Typical Jersey. Sent to Master Stuart [?] of Sutton, Surrey...

'Dear Stuart,
We are having a ripping time. It was raining when we got here but it has cleared up this afternoon & the sun is glorious. It's a fine place; we walked out over the stepping stones to Elizabeth Castle this afternoon, when the tide was out. What do you think of this "wee boo".   Love Nellie'

(Foot, Jersey)

212.

44 — JERSEY - Une Fermière - Milkmaid & Cow

235. Milkmaid and cow. Note the muslin draped over the neck of the milk can in order to filter out foreign bodies.

G. B.

40 — JERSEY - Milkmaïd and Cow

236. Milkmaid and cow. Note the fine pair of horns on this cow. Postmarked 1910.

'My dearest Ones,

I've sent so many cards that I can't remember what you've all had so if I'm duplicating you must forgive me. Now that I have broken into my second week the time will soon be gone this time next week. I'll be seeing you. Frank & Tom left for Bournemouth this morning they found it too dull here... All the people that were here when I first arrived have gone now, and we are only eight, but a jolly crowd. Am bringing some snaps of Jersey to show you, but you want to see the colouring to really appreciate it. Heaps of love to you both dears.

Yours ever, Evie'

237. Sent to Mr J McCann of Switzerland in 1937:

'I hope you like this little Jersey cow, they have such sweet faces & are very gentle, they are left to graze tied up to a stump. We are having perfectly lovely weather here, & have been able to spend a lot of time on the beach, & enjoy sunbathing. I suppose you are finding it v. hot? Are you able to bathe? We are supposed to leave at the end of the week, but I doubt that we shall. Please remember me to friends.

With love M.M.'

237. 'Truly Rural'

238. A Jersey cow.

239. Jersey cows. (Valentine & Sons., Dundee and London)

and Jersey Potatoes...

From Ward Lock's Guide, 1937:

'During the potato season the Esplanade presents a marvellous sight in the evening. Hundreds of wagons and carts enter it from the country, and almost block the traffic, although the road has a width of from 50 to 60 feet. And it is worth going to the Pier after dinner to see the mountains of barrels, brought by the vehicles, being put on board the steamer by a crane which lifts twenty-four tubs at a time...

Some few years ago the farmers gave up nearly everything for potato culture, and stupendous quantities are now exported from the Island in May, June and July. The second crop of potatoes is consumed in the Island, unless exceptionally high prices encourage exportation.

Next in importance come Tomatoes, which constitute almost as extensive a crop as potatoes. Most are produced in the open, not under glass as in Guernsey'

242   JERSEY. — *Peasants getting in potatos.* — LL.

240. Peasants getting in potatoes.
Six 'peasants', with a variety of headgear, gathering spuds in an unusually large field.
(L.L. Printed in France)

241. A Jersey Potato Field.

242. Weighbridge during Potato Season.
(Published by F.F., Jersey)

243. Postmarked 1911, a date by which the apple orchards and related cider industry which once dominated the island's agriculture had largely been replaced by Jersey potatoes.

244. 'A Jersey Farmyard'. Note the cornstack on the right supported by staddle stones. (No attribution but 'Printed in Bavaria')

245. 'Seaweed Gatherers, Le Hocq'. Known locally as *vraic*, farmers collected seaweed to spread on their fields as fertiliser. This view shows Le Hocq Common, sometime in the 1900s, an open space which became the site of St. Clement's Parish Hall. (Goodman & Sons, Birmingham)

246. 'Vraic Harvest'. (Albert Smith, phot., Jersey)

Cabbage Walking Sticks, Jersey.

The Jersey Cabbage was used primarily as cattle feed. Not much celebrated today, its extraordinarily long and tough stalk was once an object of wonder. Visitors were told that nowhere else in the world did cabbages grow so tall, least of all in Guernsey! Tourists were tempted to purchase a Jersey cabbage walking stick as a souvenir of their stay in the island...

248. Jersey Cabbages. This young lady and her milk can appear to be the same as those in no.234. (Foot)

※

249. Postmarked July 5th, 1911, addressed to Mrs Day of Forest Gate, London, the politically incorrect message reads as follows:

247. 'Cabbage Walking Sticks'.
A small boy employed by the photographer to emphasise the gigantic cabbage stalks fashioned into walking sticks.
(F. Frith & Co. Reigate)

'Dear Ma & all,
Fancy me having pluck enough to come to Jersey. Em, Daisy and I are here for the day. The weather is enough to kill a black. Crowds of Froggies here today. There is a French Band Contest.

Love Elsie'

(Peacock Post Card. The Pictorial Stationery Co., London)

※

From Ward Lock's Guide, 1920:
'The craving evinced by visitors for Jersey Cabbage Walking Stocks is known as the "Jersey fever". Nearly all holiday-makers succumb.'

248. Jersey Cabbages

249. Jersey Cabbages

227. St. Peters Vineries.
The Jersey vinery was most often a lean-to glasshouse attached to the farmhouse, and was more widespread in Guernsey than Jersey. The good crop of grapes shown here is underplanted with geraniums and other more exotic plant species.
(Valentine's)

Message to Miss A Rudge of Brixton, London, in 1937:

'Dear Rudgy

Having a lovely time. Weather is lovely too. We had a nice cold boat trip coming over. We are staying on a farm so everything is home-made and home-grown.

Love from Millie'

Oddities

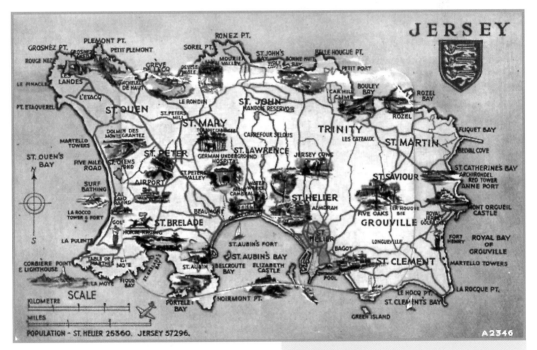

251. This full colour card features an attractive map of the island with lots of detail and all of it accurate, as far as I can see – note the population figures for St Helier and for the Island. The centre opens out to reveal a concertina of 12 individual back and white views. Postmarked 17th August, 1956, addressed to G T Esq. of Axmouth in Devon:

'Dear Daddy
I hope your foot is much better. I am going to swim most of the day with Clarke children in the swimming pool. They are very keen on swimming. We went to tea with Clarkes yesterday and they are very nice. We went for a drive in his car to some of the places we hadn't been to.'

(Valentine's "Mail Novelty")

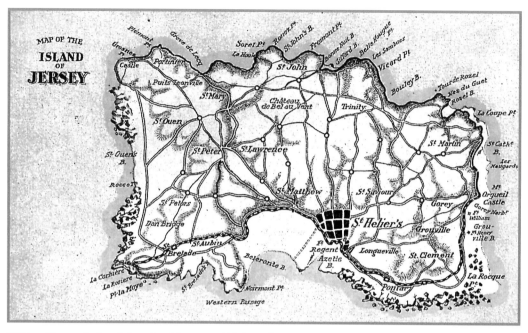

252. Map of the Island of Jersey. With a few inaccuracies, eg. 'Beleronte Bay' for Belcroute Bay. But the 12 parishes are named, and prominence given to the two railway lines from St Helier.
(J. & S. Ltd. T. on T. Printed in Saxony. Jay em jay series GY [does GY stand for Guernsey?])

253. The Channel Island and the Coast of France. Note the inset picture captioned 'Natives of Jersey'. We've already had 'Peasants' (no. 218) and here we have 'Natives'. I suppose some visitors tended to regard Jersey and her inhabitants in much the same way as they regarded the colonies.
(Published by A.J. Potts, Newport, I. of W. from Map by J. Bartholomew, Edinburgh. The "Garden Isle" Series).

This card was sent in 1903 to Miss Lilian A De Gruchy of Grove Street, St Helier and on it is written the following piece of doggerel:

> When you'll go from Jersey
> To France or Alderney,
> Granville or St. Malo,
> Carteret or Ecréhos,
> Lessay or St. Sauveur,
> You cannot do better
> Than take this card with you
> 'Twill teach you think of me, and
> Serve you on your way too
> When you will older be.

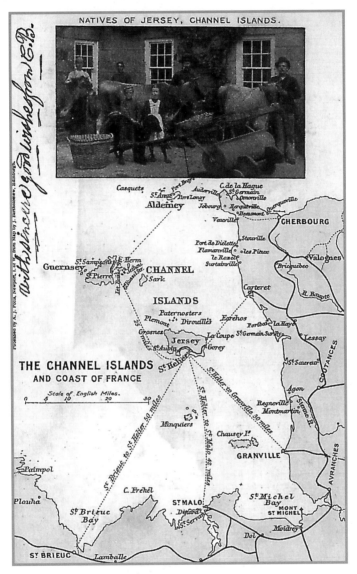

'Natives of Jersey'

The promise of pretty girls and romance was always a possibility on holiday, as these three postcards testify...

254.

(All three from the Milton "Localized" Series, published by Woolstone Bros., London, E.C.) The cards were available everywhere and simply overprinted with the names of particular resorts. The originals are attractively printed in colour.

255.

256.

257. This elaborate postcard, produced to mark the Coronation of Queen Elizabeth II in 1952, is a 'Nine View Mechanical' from Dennis Production, though the copyright was held by 'Leader Sales, Bagot, Jersey'. The nine views are black and white pictures tinted with blue. In addition to the four Jersey views in each quadrant, and the picture of the Royal couple, the windscreen wiper shaped aperture at the top reveals a further four views when the wheel is rotated – the wheel's axle is the unidentified flying object between the Queen and the Duke. This card is unused and was no doubt purchased as a souvenir of the historic moment. I doubt anything similar was produced to mark the Golden Jubilee in 2002.

257. Sent 2nd August,1958, addressed to Mr & Mrs S of Mordy, Monmouthshire:

'Having a grand time, the weather is good, not too cold. New biro hope you can understand. Just off for a walk up town.   Isobel & Tony'

(Valentine & Sons., Dundee and London)

Message on card sent to Miss Brouard in Guernsey, 1904:

Dear Con

We are just back before the storm it is raining & thundering. We have been at St Aubin's for the day since ten this morning the children have enjoyed the bathing it was lovely only Oh so hot. Franky don't want to go home again. He would like to live here. Hope you're all well.

Annie

JERSEY-S.S. "LYDIA" LE DÉPART – S.S. "LYDIA" LEAVING JERSEY SHORE

259. S.S. *Lydia* leaving Jersey shore. People gathered at the end of Albert Pier to see off friends and relations, or perhaps just the boat and its passengers, as she steams towards Elizabeth Castle Breakwater. It was once a favourite occupation of some Jersey folk to stroll down the pier in order to welcome or bid farewell to the mailboat and its passengers.
(F.F Jersey)

Message sent 23 April, 1907:

Tuesday

Such a nice calm day to-day & there doesn't seem to be much wind, I hope it will be calm to-morrow. I will telegraph from London, so if you don't hear, you will know it was too frisky.

Best love V.W.S.

Index

Postcards referred to in this book are cited by card number, rather than page number

*John Le Dain, compiler of this
book, some years ago.*

More titles from Seaflower Books, all priced at between £4.95 and £9.95 ~

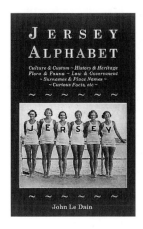

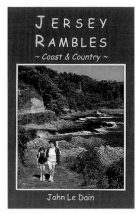

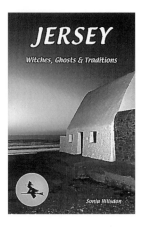

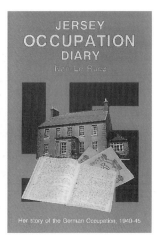

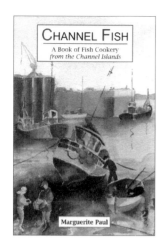

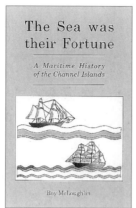

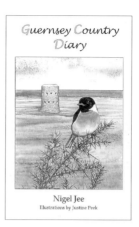

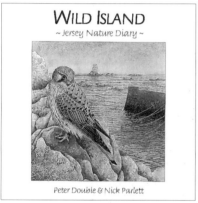

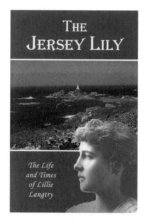

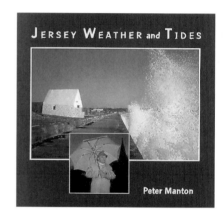

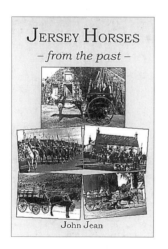